Finely Tuned:

How to Thrive as a Highly Sensitive Person or Empath

Barrie Davenport

ISBN:1515023354
ISBN-13:9781515023357

Disclaimer

Your Free Gift

As a way of saying thank you for your purchase, I hope you'll enjoy 39 Power Habits of Wildly Successful People. These are daily and weekly habits you can incorporate in your life to support your inner work as a highly sensitive person or empath. These habits will improve your health, your relationships, your personal growth, and your career success. Prioritize the habits most important to you, and begin working on them one by one. I hope you enjoy this free book.

Download this free report by going to this website:

https://barriedavenport.leadpages.net/39-habits-signup/

Contents

About Barrie Davenport

Barrie Davenport is a certified personal coach, thought leader, author, and creator of several online courses on self-confidence, life passion, and habit creation. She is the founder of two top-ranked personal development sites, LiveBoldandBloom.com and BarrieDavenport.com. Her work as a coach, blogger, and author is focused on offering people practical strategies for living happier, more successful, and more mindful lives. She utilizes time-tested, evidence based, action-oriented principles and methods to create real and measurable results for self-improvement.

You can learn more about Barrie on her Amazon author page at barriedavenport.com/author.

Introduction

The finest qualities of our nature, like the bloom on fruits, can be preserved only by the most delicate handling. Yet we do not treat ourselves nor one another thus tenderly.

~ Henry David Thoreau

Upheaval and discord were frequent visitors in my house while I was growing up. My parents, who were a mismatch from the start, had frequent and loud arguments fueled by too much alcohol. When they weren't arguing, there was a simmering tension and unhappiness that settled between them.

My older half-siblings were teenagers when I was young, and their teenage angst and drama was exacerbated by our parent's discord, in addition to having two new sisters (my older sister and me) who now required my parents' time and attention. Having lost their biological mother to cancer when they were small, my older half-siblings expressed their pain and confusion dramatically in their teen years with door slamming, yelling, and disobedience.

As a small and silent witness to this chaos, I learned quickly to remain quiet, compliant, and out of the way. I was exceedingly conscientious and tried hard to please so I wouldn't trigger any anger or drama. The less I added to the turmoil, the better it would be for everyone—especially for me. Had I possessed a different personality, perhaps this strategy would have worked well. I could have kept quiet and out of the way, and walked away relatively unscathed. Or I could have joined in and allowed my fear and anger an outlet, rather than hiding and repressing my feelings.

Fortunately, it wasn't chaos all the time. There were periods of normalcy and calm, and despite the tension and eruptions, I knew my parents and siblings loved me. But even during these calm times, I remained alert and on edge, scanning the emotional landscape to sense any looming eruptions.

The problem for me was that I *felt* everything so keenly. I could easily read expressions, the nuances of a mood shift, and the energy in the room. I absorbed tension like an emotional sponge, which made me suffer terribly. Recognizing my mother's deep sadness, even when she appeared happy, I felt responsible for her well-being and wanted to protect her. I instinctively knew when bad things were going to happen, and I was constantly hypervigilant, always waiting for the next shoe to drop.

In addition to reacting to subtle energies, I was more sensitive and reactive to loud noise and overstimulation or excitement. Witnessing or hearing arguments and anger was painful and disturbing. If any tension or anger were specifically directed at me, I was quick to change my behavior or apologize in order to regain emotional equilibrium. I got my feelings hurt easily and was thrown off-balance when someone would say something critical or unkind.

I did everything in my youthful power to prevent arguments within my family before they erupted or to cut them off when I saw them brewing. Of course this was beyond my capacity, but it didn't go unnoticed by my family who referred to me as "the little peacemaker." In fact, I craved peace and a loving, calm environment where everyone just got along—or at least could work out their differences in a less dramatic fashion.

Fortunately, I also felt positive emotions quite deeply. I felt intense love for my parents, became strongly attached to my friends, enjoyed hugs and physical affection, and was deeply moved by touching stories, art, or music. Since I responded to the moods and needs of others, I was able to solidify strong friendships, and I instinctively knew how to pull the right groups of people together.

Even though I cherished my friendships, I was always the girl at sleepovers to go to bed early and find a quiet place to pull my sleeping bag away from the late-night chatter of my friends. I was the teenager leaving the party well before midnight or pulling away from the crowd to have a quiet conversation with someone. I was the conscientious "goody two shoes," reminding my friends that we might get in trouble if we played a prank or made a typically stupid teenage decision. I was also the person my friends gravitated toward when they needed advice or comfort.

As I grew older and lived on my own, I discovered other interesting sensitivities. When life got too intense, or if I was overstimulated, I needed to withdraw and spend time alone. I was more sensitive than most of my friends to medication, caffeine, crowded and noisy environments, and making major life changes. My intense feelings around conflict, arguing, and violence never abated.

On more occasions than I can count, I've heard the words, "Don't be so sensitive" from friends and romantic partners. These words always left me confused and stung, as though I had some character flaw. I assumed everyone felt things as intensely as I did and couldn't understand the casual reactions others had to situations that left me reeling for days.

As I've gotten older and understood more about highly sensitive people and empaths, I've learned to manage and appreciate my own sensitivities. I've learned how to protect myself and design my lifestyle to support these natural personality traits. While I've found some sensitivities have gotten less intense over time (getting my feelings hurt so easily, for example), other sensitivities have grown more intense. I can't tolerate loud and noisy environments for very long. I find the lighting, visual stimulation, and noise in malls extremely unpleasant. I'm even less inclined to tolerate or expose myself to people who have "negative energy" and who seem to enjoy drama and conflict.

Before I learned about highly sensitive people, I thought something was wrong with me. Because so many people remarked about my being "too sensitive," I assumed I was the misfit and needed to toughen up and get over it. I didn't respect "the finest qualities of our nature," as Thoreau so aptly defines our sensitivities. Nor did I treat myself tenderly, and I accepted people in my life who didn't treat me tenderly either.

Now, however, I view my sensitive nature as a gift—one that has allowed me to explore a depth of feeling and a rich inner life that nonsensitives don't appear to savor. I am deeply moved by art, poetry and prose, dance, music, and nature. My relationships are intimate and rewarding. Having learned the best type of people, work, activities, and environments that suit my nature, I've been able to design my life to enhance the positive aspects of my sensitivities and minimize the negative. This has taken time, considerable effort, and continual self-awareness.

Much scientific research and study has been conducted on the sensitivity trait, most notably by Dr. Elaine Aron, a pioneer in researching highly sensitive people (HSP). The main focus of this book is on HSPs and how to thrive as a sensitive person.

However, I discuss the traits of empaths extensively in Chapter 7 and in other chapters of the book. The terms "highly sensitive person" and "empath" are often confused or used interchangeably in the media and on blogs and sites about sensitivity. Although the two are not the same, there are many traits shared by both empaths and HSPs, and it's important to understand the similarities and distinctions between them.

Those who consider themselves empaths will benefit tremendously from understanding HSP traits and learning how to use the life strategies presented throughout this book. Those who are strictly HSPs will understand how empaths suffer the same misunderstandings and internal pain as their HSP cousins. Both personalities can learn to embrace the positive aspects of their unique natures and to manage their environments and relationships in order to live happily.

However, being a highly sensitive person or an empath can be lonely and confusing. There are far more nonsensitives in the world than there are highly sensitive people and empaths. Because we are outnumbered, and the majority of people aren't likely to intuit our particular needs, it's up to us to design our lives so we can thrive in a world that doesn't share all our sensitivities.

We can't and shouldn't *expect* others to understand the unique qualities of our sensitive natures. However, we can and should try to share information about our sensitive traits with those close to us so they better understand who we are and why we respond the way we do. Also, we must learn to accept that those around us aren't necessarily being insensitive when our sensitivities are offended. We are called to understand the true motivations of non-HSPs, just as we want them to understand and accept us.

Only through self-awareness and open dialogue with others can we function optimally, using our sensitive natures to guide us to mutual respect in relationships and mindful self-care in our environments. It is for this reason I've written this book—to help you function optimally in a world that often feels overwhelming and painful.

As a fellow HSP and empath-sympathizer, I want to offer a guidebook to assist you on your personal journey as a sensitive, empathic person. Navigating your way through this complicated world, with all its noise, distractions, and insensitivities, can be daunting and bewildering. However, once you learn more about your true nature and implement some coping strategies for your life, you'll be free to enjoy your heightened sensitivities and savor the richness of experience they afford you.

Chapter 1: What Is an HSP?

Early in the 20th century, Swiss psychiatrist Carl Jung researched innate archetypal psychic dispositions that make up the collective unconscious (structures of the unconscious mind that are shared among all people). One of the dispositions he determined was "innate sensitiveness," the trait of high sensitivity. Jung thought this innate sensitiveness predisposed some people to be especially impacted by negative or traumatic childhood experiences, so much so that in adulthood they have more difficulty adapting and coping when faced with a particular challenge.

> Events bound up with powerful impressions can never pass off without leaving some trace on sensitive people. Some of them remain effective throughout life, and such events can have a determining influence on a person's whole mental development.
>
> ~ C. G. Jung

Jung, an HSP, also noticed the positive aspects of being a highly sensitive person, especially during times of relative calm and equanimity. He recognized that sensitiveness was not a personality disorder but often an advantageous trait that can enhance one's experience of life in the right circumstances.

This excessive sensitiveness very often brings an
enrichment of the personality. . . . Only, when
difficult and unusual situations arise, the advantage
frequently turns into a very great disadvantage,
since calm consideration is then disturbed by
untimely affects. Nothing could be more mistaken,
though, than to regard this excessive sensitiveness
as in itself a pathological character component. If
that were really so, we should have to rate about
one quarter of humanity as pathological.

~ C. G. Jung

Decades later, dozens of other researchers confirmed Jung's
findings, and one researcher in particular, Dr. Aron, has made an
invaluable contribution to the field of knowledge about HSPs. She
is a pioneer in studying sensitivity using functional magnetic
resonance imaging (MRI) to determine what happens in the brains
of highly sensitive people.

Dr. Aron began her research on innate sensitiveness in 1991,
analyzing three areas of inquiry she pinpointed in her work: (1) the
greater sensitivity of introverts, (2) the innate reactivity of a large
minority of infants, and (3) biologists' descriptions of a similar trait
in numerous animal species. "I was encouraged to try to develop a
measure to identify and study those with this trait, whatever its
final name," says Dr. Aron in a 2006 article for the *Journal of
Jungian Theory and Practice.*

Dr. Aron confirms that high sensitivity, also called sensory-
processing sensitivity, is an innate trait in which people notice
more subtleties and process information more deeply. But this
definition only touches the surface of how these sensitivities
manifest.

On her website, The Highly Sensitive Person (hsperson.com), Dr. Aron says,

> Highly sensitive people are typically good listeners, need more down time, are bothered by noisy or crowded places, may want to do novel things all day (they can be high sensation seekers) but then want to go rest in the evening, notice things that others miss, cry easily, are upset more than others by injustices, feel more joy and compassion, are conscientious and loyal, fussy too, tolerate caffeine poorly, feel pain more, are slow to make decisions, and see the larger consequences of plans and actions.

Dr. Aron defines the core qualities of the highly sensitive person in her blog, "How Do You Recognize an HSP?" using the acronym DOES:

Depth of Processing

- Unusual, creative ideas
- Extraordinarily conscientious
- Prefers to decide things slowly and mull things over
- Decisions are often correct

Overstimulated Easily

- More easily stressed by noise, chaotic situations, and deadlines
- Seeks quiet spots
- Prefers to work alone or at home

- Needs more downtime

Emotionally Reactive

- Reacts strongly to feedback, both positive and negative

- Cries easily

- Shows considerable empathy for others

- Worries more about others' reactions to negative events

- Offers more positive feedback to others

- Becomes angry, curious, sad, anxious, or joyful sooner than others

Sensitive to Subtle Stimuli

- Notices details and things that others don't

- Arranges home and work spaces with special care, such as adjusting the lighting

- Comments on others' clothing or small changes in the environment or weather

In Western culture, hypersensitivity is often viewed as a character flaw, but during the past few decades, Dr. Aron and other researchers have proven it to be less of a personal defect and more the result of neurological activity that creates a preference to process information differently. HSPs simply experience more activity in certain parts of the brain.

In a study published in *Brain and Behavior,* researchers scanned the brains of 18 married individuals (some with high sensitivity and some with low sensitivity) while they viewed photos of either smiling or sad faces. One group of photos included faces of strangers, and the other included photos of their husbands or wives.

In response to the findings, Dr. Aron reported,

> We found that areas of the brain involved with awareness and emotion, particularly those areas connected with empathetic feelings, in the highly sensitive people showed substantially greater blood flow to relevant brain areas than was seen in individuals with low sensitivity during the twelve second period when they viewed the photos.

Unfortunately, many highly sensitive people aren't aware of this research, nor do they understand why they feel so different. The vast majority of HSPs have likely never heard of the trait, much less think of it as something normal. Highly sensitive people often try to hide their sensitive traits and alter their behavior and choices in order to fit in and appear normal.

If you are an HSP and have often been criticized or teased about your nature, you've probably also masked these traits. Maybe you've been labeled shy, a cry baby, overly emotional, or too intense. More than likely, most of the people around you don't quite understand you and your reactions. Maybe others don't know your true nature because you hide it so well.

Dana, a reader who commented on a post about HSPs on my blog Live Bold and Bloom.com, acknowledges the misunderstandings about the trait, both in herself and from others. "A lot of these traits are things that I knew about myself, but not necessarily things I understood," says Dana.

I've been accused of being overly sensitive and walled off. I've had people come into my life who claimed to love me and then want to help 'fix' me because it's not normal to be so protective of my tender heart. I see now that it's more likely that I am a person with HSP, and that I'm really okay.

It really *is* okay to be an HSP as you will learn through this book, but understanding this multifaceted trait can be daunting, as it's difficult to wrap the highly sensitive personality into one tidy definition. If I had to offer a description to cover it all, I'd say HSPs are "finely tuned" (hence the name of this book). We may be wired a bit tighter and require more maintenance, but our emotional instrument is uniquely rich and complex.

Yes, we need regular calibration and tender loving care (from ourselves and others) in order to function at our highest and most creative levels. But when we learn to manage our reactions and environments appropriately, we will enjoy deeply satisfying experiences of joy, intuition, creativity, and compassion—all of which can make a profound and positive impact on the world around us.

Chapter 2: Am I Normal?

I still feel like I need help to overcome or help understand myself more. I feel lost at times because others I'm around in my work area aren't the same as me. I try to fit in but it doesn't feel like me.

When I went to high school, it was a nightmare!
I was an outcast from every group dynamic.

It sucked being weird. Being told to get over it. It's still embarrassing for me to cry at the drop of a hat over TV, books, things people say.

I have also suffered from being the outcast, feeling constantly harshly criticized. In school, no one would associate with me— even teachers bullied me.

These comments are from readers on my blog, both men and women, expressing their experiences as highly sensitive people. Until they recognized themselves as HSPs, they thought they were abnormal, different, and flawed in some way. When the world is telling you that your emotions and reactions aren't "normal" or acceptable, you begin to believe it. Either you work hard to fit in and change your behavior, or you isolate yourself to avoid the feelings of shame, confusion, and pain.

The stories from my readers reflect more the norm than the exception for HSPs, especially in American culture where toughness, emotional control, and the ability to "just get over it" are expected and even revered. This is especially true for men, who are viewed as weak and unmanly if they cry, show excessive emotion, or "overreact." Being a highly sensitive man presents unique difficulties, as men are held to a standard of masculinity and strength that does not pair well with a deeply sensitive nature.

Says blogger and HSP Peter Messerschmidt in a post on sensitive men:

> I feel that that modern society—especially in the United States—has created a set of cultural ideals that make it *particularly* difficult for Highly Sensitive Men to *learn* about, and come to *terms* with, and then be *open* and *honest* about their sensitivity.

> Apart from the many who simply *ignore* the possibility that they might be an HSM, I feel certain there are also significant numbers who may be *aware* of their sensitivity, but feel hesitant or afraid that anyone else might find out—even their families and loved ones. . . .

> As a result, it is highly likely that many HS Men live lives of "quiet suffering—" many choosing to mask and "narcoticize" the pain of "not fitting the male ideal" with alcohol, drugs, sex, gambling or other addictions.

Women are biologically hard-wired to be more sensitive, empathic, and intuitive, but are often labeled as moody, hysterical, or unbalanced if the scales tip too far into the unacceptable range of sensitivity. Says New York psychiatrist Julie Holland in a February 2015 article for the *New York Times*, "Women's emotionality is a sign of health, not disease; it is a source of power. But we are under constant pressure to restrain our emotional lives. We have been taught to apologize for our tears, to suppress our anger and to fear being called hysterical."

Very little in modern Western society is set up to support highly sensitive people. The International Management Facility Association estimates that 70 percent of American employees work in open-plan environments where there is an abundance of stimulation, noise, and distractions. American employees only use 51 percent of their eligible paid vacation time and paid time off, according to a recent survey by research firm Harris Interactive of 2,300 workers who receive paid vacation. They don't take the time off because they fear getting behind in their work or being outperformed by their colleagues.

The traits of the Type A personality, such as ambition, competitiveness, and time urgency are qualities that are highly valued in American society. American workers take less vacation time than any other industrialized country in the world, and we often take our work with us on holidays. We are encouraged to create adrenaline-fueled lifestyles that are task-oriented, fast-paced, and jam-packed with activities and obligations—so we appear productive and valuable. Even our downtime is excessively stimulating, as we're constantly connected to cell phones, computers, and televisions.

This pace of life is stressful for anyone, but for the highly sensitive person, it's unsustainable and unhealthy. Yet try telling this to your boss or your peers and see how they respond. Who's going to understand your need for a calm, quiet work environment or the extra time you require to process information? Who will reward you for craving more downtime and taking all your vacation? Who will see it as a virtue to drop unnecessary obligations or commitments in favor of just doing nothing?

The best thing you can do for yourself and the people in your closest circles is to educate yourself about your unique personality and processing preferences—and why you are as "normal" as anyone around you. Then you'll be prepared to educate others and to make the life changes necessary to allow you to thrive and feel confident about who you are.

Who you are is NOT an aberration. In fact, a large body of research has confirmed that innate sensitivity is found in 15 to 20 percent of the population. According to Dr. Aron, this percentage is too large for high sensitivity to be classified as a disorder. Unfortunately, it's just small enough that it's not well understood or accepted by the majority of other people.

High sensory processing sensitivity has been frequently confused and associated with shyness, problems with social anxiety, and phobia, fearfulness, and introversion. Although some HSPs express these behaviors, they are not innate or universal among all highly sensitive people. In fact, 30 percent of HSPs are extraverts, and the seeming shyness expressed by HSPs is often a result of their preference to look and process before entering new situations.

Other research in developmental psychology offers even more evidence that people naturally differ in their sensitivities. According to the differential susceptibility hypothesis developed by Jay Belsky, PhD, director of the Institute for the Study of Children, Families, and Social Issues and professor of psychology at Birkbeck University of London, people vary in the degrees they're affected by experiences or the environments they are exposed to.

Some individuals are more sensitive to these influences than others, both the negative and positive influences.

Biologists have even found the trait in more than 100 other species, including fruit flies, birds, fish, dogs, cats, horses, and primates. It appears high sensitivity is an evolutionary trait that reflects a type of survival strategy—being observant and thoughtful before acting. Those with the highly sensitive trait in any species are always in the minority, but it seems they might give the species an evolutionary advantage, as they tend to process situations with their brains first, while others rush to act. This can be advantageous to the entire group in situations when a thoughtful, measured approach is more suitable or less dangerous.

Highly sensitive people are valuable and important to their communities and to the world at large. Because of your strong intuition and ability to sense what others don't, you are often the first line of defense (or offense) in helping those around you. You are the shamans, the mediators, the counselors, the physicians, and the healers that all societies for thousands of years have required for their survival.

What HSPs Are Not

To summarize, I want you to be clear that being an HSP doesn't mean you have a psychological disorder. High sensitivity doesn't make you shy or neurotic, nor does it necessarily indicate introversion. To clarify the differences in these conditions, let's examine them more closely:

Shyness

Shyness is a feeling of timidity, apprehension, or discomfort in some social situations, and it's a learned behavior. HSPs are often labeled as "shy" because they prefer to observe and hold back before entering new situations. However, this isn't caused by fear or aversion but rather the need to process new sensory data more deeply than most.

Neurosis

Neurosis is a mild behavior disorder that isn't caused by an organic disease. People with neuroticism tend to suffer with a number of affective disorders, such as anxiety, depression, and obsessive states. HSPs are susceptible to some of these disorders as a result of the overwhelm they feel to past events or current stimuli. Other people might not understand this underlying cause and will view the HSP as neurotic, but the condition has a real and physiological cause to the HSP.

Introversion

Although the majority of HSPs are introverts, the two are not the same. Introversion is a personality trait in which people are focused primarily on the inner world of the mind and enjoy exploring their thoughts and feelings. Introverts need to spend time alone to energize them. Too much time with others is draining. They tend to be quiet, reserved, and introspective. Not all HSPs have this trait, and even those that do might desire to be more social, but they feel overwhelmed in certain social situations.

So going back to the question, "Am I normal?"—the answer is an unqualified "Yes." High sensitivity is part of the normal spectrum of human responsiveness. You are as normal as any of your less-sensitive friends, although they outnumber you. That's why it's so vitally important you embrace yourself as a highly sensitive person and educate those in your personal and professional life about how the trait is beneficial to you and to them.

Chapter 3: The HSP Self-Assessment

I too am hypersensitive and have just recently learned that this is a part of my personality that I should not be ashamed of. I have been in relationships that start off great but then I'm accused of being too sensitive. I now embrace it and let people know that being hypersensitive is not a bad thing. I mostly had to learn this on my own but not without being riddled with pain, isolation and feeling there is something really wrong with me. I think this is something that should be talked about more and become more mainstreamed.

~ Mechele, reader at Live Bold and Bloom

Thank you for this article Barrie, and your readers for the comments. I thought "Eureka!" when I saw this. It's like hitting a milestone in that journey of self-discovery. I am from Kenya and it's nice to know that this personality is global. I wish more people would read this article and know what we know now. Maybe they would find it easier to understand themselves and the people around them. It would surely improve a lot of interpersonal relationships. I have nothing but gratitude, keep doing this."

~ Elie, reader at Live Bold and Bloom

It is hugely liberating as an HSP when you finally realize you aren't crazy or abnormal and that there are other people who share your highly sensitive nature. Many HSPs live through most of their adult lives not understanding themselves and feeling different and isolated. So many readers on my blog expressed their relief and appreciation in the comments of posts I've written about highly sensitive people. They didn't know what was "wrong" with them until they learned about the trait.

Unfortunately, many HSPs have experienced depression, anxiety, and relationship problems as a result of not understanding themselves, being maligned by family and others in their lives, and by making poor choices that don't support their sensitive personalities. In their struggles to conform or protect themselves, they have lived compromised lives.

Through a lack of awareness and understanding, they've failed to create coping strategies or build a life that works best for their innate natures. They choose relationships with people who are on the far end of the sensitivity scale, leaving both people confused and unhappy. They've tried to shove down, diminish, and hide their sensitivities and have essentially denied who they really are in order to fit in.

All this is so unfortunate and unnecessary, when the highly sensitive nature should be celebrated and respected. The first step toward changing your self-perception and the perceptions of those around you is awareness. As you are reading this book (and because you chose this book), you likely see yourself as a highly sensitive person—or maybe there's a highly sensitive person in your life.

Dr. Aron has developed an assessment to confirm whether or not you are a highly sensitive person. You can take the assessment

by answering the questions at this site:
http://hsperson.com/test/highly-sensitive-test/.

If you are just discovering that you or someone close to
you is a highly sensitive person, the good news is that you
now have unlocked the door to understanding more about
why you (or someone you know) react and behave the way
you do. It's true, HSPs are the minority, and, as such, they
might consider themselves "abnormal" or different. The
reality is that HSPs have many wonderful, positive qualities
due to the makeup of their nervous systems.

These include the following traits:

- Creativity

- Compassion

- Empathy

- Focus

- Thoughtfulness

- Loyalty

- Attention to detail

- Awareness of subtleties

- Calmness

- Spirituality

- Contemplation

- Diplomacy

- Intuition

- Sense of justice

- Harmony

- Purpose-oriented

- Idealism

- Innovative

- Collaborative

- Wisdom

- Gentle strength

- Peacefulness

- Insightfulness

- Conscientiousness

- Reverence for nature and beauty

As you address some of the more difficult aspects of being a highly sensitive person, remember you have some extraordinary traits that more than make up for the difficulties. When you learn to manage your environment, daily choices, and lifestyle, you can choose to play to these strengths in order to optimize them and your enjoyment of life. All people, whether or not they are highly sensitive, have strengths and weaknesses. Choose to focus on your strengths as a sensitive, while you build strategies to manage your weaknesses.

Chapter 4: Physical Reactions and Traits

My parents would fight and I would get physically ill.
Mostly in my stomach.

~ Shaun, reader at Live Bold and Bloom

As an HSP, your body and your body awareness are more finely tuned than most others. You might have physical reactions and discomforts that nonsensitives don't experience or don't feel so intensely. I've noticed this phenomenon in myself in many situations. One too many cups of coffee in the morning can shift my mood from high-energy and upbeat to anxious and agitated. Over the years, I've learned to combine decaf and caffeinated coffee and to drink no more than two cups in the morning—with food.

I'm also highly aware of changes or pains in my body and tend to respond more acutely to specific medications. I've had doctors suggest I was overreacting to pain during certain procedures that I found excruciating. The combination of the pain and the shame of experiencing so much pain made these experiences even more difficult, something you eventually try to avoid altogether.

"Naturally unbearable pain leads to a fear of experiencing anything like it ever again, and that creates a complex about it," says Dr. Aron on her blog. "The complex can make us overly afraid of injury, medical procedures, a long illness, or the experience of dying."

On the positive side, I have a profoundly favorable reaction to physical affection and massage. It's as though my skin craves touch, and physical touch immediately relaxes me. I also find I'm noticeably calmer and more physically relaxed when I'm in nature, particularly walking in the mountains or on the beach. I can be around people who instantly put me at ease, and others who immediately make me feel anxious and stressed.

As a highly sensitive person, you might notice some of these same physical reactions and traits in yourself:

- Being more aware than others of physical changes and symptoms

- Having highly refined sensory details

- Experiencing skin rashes, redness, and reactions to chemicals

- Having acute sensitivity to touch

- Having strong negative reactions to loud or repetitive noises

- Feeling distracted or disturbed by sounds that others don't notice, like a ticking clock or people talking in the background

- Noticing subtle details around you and being able to find lost things more readily than others

Finely Tuned

- Being highly sensitive to strong light, or preferring natural light to artificial

- Feeling overwhelmed by unpleasant smells and perfumes and needing fresh air

- Having a sophisticated, subtle palette or having strong distaste for certain foods

- Experiencing more acute reactions to pain and pleasure than others

- Experiencing more acute reactions to medications

- Strongly affected by stimulants, such as caffeine and sugar, and by depressants, such as alcohol

- Physically agitated by intense environments, such as malls, concerts, or airports

- Experiencing chemical sensitivity to food additives, dyes, perfumes, and household products

- Having keen fine motor skills

- Experiencing a weaker immune system, often due to the stress of overstimulation

- Needing more sleep than other people

- Having greater reaction to or awareness of changes in the natural environment, such as a shift in barometric pressure or the onset of seasonal changes

- Having physical reactions to emotional turmoil or stress around you, such as feeling ill when someone is angry around you

As HSPs, we have nervous systems that tune in to subtle experiences and react to them more dramatically, either positively or negatively. Our keen awareness of our bodies and the reactions our bodies have to certain stimuli make it necessary for us to be more mindful of how we treat ourselves. It's important for everyone to eat healthy pure food, to drink lots of water, and to exercise. It's even more essential for highly sensitive people in order to maintain physical and emotional equilibrium. We need to use our keen awareness to understand what our bodies are telling us and how we can alter our lifestyle choices in order to allow our bodies to function optimally.

Think about how your own body reacts to experiences, people, environments, food, drink, medications, sounds, smells, chemicals, stress, lack of sleep, and pain. Begin with the most debilitating physical reaction you experience, something that disrupts your life or makes you extremely uncomfortable, and take action to address it. This might mean going to your doctor, eliminating or cutting back on certain foods, going to bed earlier, or avoiding certain places or people. There is nothing wrong with you because you have physical reactions and needs that others don't. Be kind to yourself, and pay attention to what your body is telling you so you can enjoy your gifts without the distractions of physical discomfort.

Chapter 5: The HSP's Childhood

For a very long time, I felt ashamed of myself for being "too sensitive." Throughout my childhood, this term was used like a weapon. I was admonished for expressing my feelings to the point that I shut them down. After a traumatic experience, I went into a deep depression since I did not have the ability or freedom to express my pain. Having had family who did not (or could not) appreciate or accept this quality, I have experienced strained relationships and self-esteem issues for many years. Only now, after having discovered and researched being a highly sensitive person, I am able to start accepting, and valuing, this rich and vibrant quality within myself.

~ Carrie, reader at Live Bold and Bloom

My childhood was riddled with examples of being ridiculed or in some cases specifically targeted (such as being sneaked up on because I startled so extremely). It certainly was not a trait that I valued and in fact, my self-esteem and confidence suffered a great deal, as I sought to deal with a volatile environment, minimize stress and seek isolation. It all felt extremely overwhelming and distressing, and I felt like such a misfit in a world that seemed not to feel the way I did.

~Shaleen, reader at Live Bold and Bloom

I felt emotionally involved in every argument even though I was just a child, and it was between my parents and not me. I tried to lose myself in reading and became a terribly quiet and withdrawn child even though I do not think I am necessarily shy.

~ Jane, reader at Live Bold and Bloom

The comments about sensing subtle changes in the mood of the house and trying to "fix things" and being the "peacemaker" really hit home. That was me all over as a young child. And I was taught that the expression of "negative" emotions, like anger, especially, was not welcomed, nor even allowed.

~ Marsha, reader at Live Bold and Bloom

Highly sensitive adults were once highly sensitive children. The childhood experiences of HSPs profoundly impact how they experience the world and cope with challenges when they reach adulthood. It's no surprise that highly sensitive children come out of the womb more intense, persistent, and demanding than other infants. If you are highly sensitive, you might have heard stories from your parents about how you behaved and reacted as a baby.

"I had to hold you all the time."

"You nursed constantly."

"You never slept!"

"You would scream your head off if we didn't rock you."

Your parents might have compared you to your calmer, easier siblings who slept through the night right away, soothed themselves happily, and didn't need constant attention. These stories alone might have made you feel different or difficult—as though your parents had to put up with you and your strange behavior as an infant.

Developmental psychologist Jerome Kagan did early research on infants and young children who were sensitive and more needy. He called this temperament trait "behavioral inhibition" (BI) and was the first to identify behavioral inhibition in children as a potential indicator of anxiety in later years. Kagan's studies reveal that BI in infants is biological and is a genetically influenced attribute. He showed that areas of the brain, primarily the amygdala, were important centers in the expression and regulation of behavioral inhibition.

Pediatrician and renowned parenting author Dr. William Sears also corroborates the research showing high sensitivity as an innate quality. He believes it's a trait that reveals itself in a baby's personality almost from the moment of birth. Sears coined the term "high needs baby" after the birth of his own fourth child, Hayden, who was more sensitive and demanding than his previous three. "Hayden became an in arms, at breast, and in our bed high needs baby," says Sears. "If we tried to leave her for a much needed baby break, she'd protest against any baby sitter."

As he continued to research high needs babies, Sears identified twelve common characteristics they share:

1. Intense: "These babies put more energy into everything they do. They cry loudly, feed voraciously, laugh with gusto, and protest more forcefully if their needs are not met to their satisfaction. Because they feel so deeply, they react more powerfully if their feelings are disturbed," say Sears.

2. Hyperactive: According to Sears, "there are some high need babies who seem to shun containment and physical contact. They stiffen their limbs and arch their backs when you try to hold them, and they are frequently seen doing back dives in your lap, turning breastfeeding into a gymnastic event."

3. Draining: Sensitive babies simply need more from their parents—more holding, more attention, more nursing, more comforting.

4. Feeds Frequently: High needs babies want to nurse more often, not just for nutrition, but also for comfort. They need their mother's breast to pacify their intense emotions.

5. Demanding: High needs babies let you know in no uncertain terms what they need. Says Sears, "These babies convey a sense of urgency in their signals; they do not like waiting, and they do not readily accept alternatives."

6. Awakens Frequently: High needs babies seem to need less sleep than other babies. They might take longer to fall asleep and awaken more in the middle of the night or early from naps.

7. Unsatisfied: There will be days the parent of a high needs baby will feel totally inadequate because nothing seems to comfort or satisfy their baby.

8. Unpredictable: High needs babies might have extreme mood swings. The comforting techniques that worked one day might be totally ineffective the next.

9. Super-Sensitive: "High need babies prefer a secure and known environment, and they are quick to protest when their equilibrium is upset," says Dr. Sears. These babies startle more easily and are highly aware of their environments and any subtle changes.

10. Can't Put Baby Down: These babies crave physical touch, motion, and skin-to-skin contact. However, some high needs babies get overstimulated with too much touch or being swaddled tightly.

11. Not a Self-Soother: High needs babies can't calm themselves with the typical soothing actions, such as sucking a pacifier or sitting in a swing. They need help to calm down and fall asleep and prefer people rather than things to help them.

12. Separation Sensitive: "These infants do not readily accept substitute care and are notoriously slow to warm up to strangers," says Dr. Sears. They feel calm when they are one with their mother and out-of-sorts when they are separated from her.

As you can see, highly sensitive babies require special parenting skills and the parents' awareness that their baby is behaving normally for his or her temperament. It can be challenging and exhausting to be the parent, particularly the mother, of a baby who requires so much time, energy, and handling. It can also be extremely distressing for the parents if they believe there's something wrong with their baby or with their own ability to parent.

For highly sensitive adults who were raised before the 1970s, your parents might have followed the more rigid parenting advice of the times, including ideas such as these: Let your baby cry himself to sleep. Don't hold her so much—you'll spoil her. Feed him on a schedule, you don't need to nurse every time he wants your breast. Never let your baby sleep with you—she'll never get out of your bed.

If this is how your parents raised you, it was likely because they were given the wrong advice about how to manage your unique needs. They learned quickly that what might work for other babies didn't work well for you. As you grew older, your infant needs didn't go away—but you might have expressed them differently. Highly sensitive children might use unusually big words, notice subtleties, and seem intuitive. They might also complain about scratchy clothing, notice unusual odors, and be bothered by crowds and noises. As a highly sensitive child, you probably felt things more deeply than other children, asked a lot of questions, and didn't need harsh correction or strong punishment to bring you back in line.

Says Dr. Aron, "Because children are a blend of a number of temperament traits, some HSCs are fairly difficult—active, emotionally intense, demanding, and persistent—while others are calm, turned inward, and almost too easy to raise except when they are expected to join a group of children they do not know. But outspoken and fussy or reserved and obedient, all HSCs are sensitive to their emotional and physical environment."

If you were a highly sensitive child born into a healthy, caring, and loving family, your sensitivities were met with understanding and patience. You weren't treated as "abnormal" but rather as a unique and gifted child to be treasured and celebrated. Your parents helped you navigate your environment and supported your needs for less stimulation. They appreciated your clever sense of humor and your ability to sense the feelings of those around you.

As a highly sensitive adult, you might still experience people who misunderstand you, but your parental support in early childhood has protected you against severe emotional distress in the face of life difficulties as you've gotten older. You are able to bounce back more quickly to life stressors and daily challenges.

If, however, you suffered emotional or physical trauma as a child, or if you were bullied, teased, or mistreated because of your sensitive nature, then you were much more affected by these difficulties in childhood than a non-HSP. As a result of your negative childhood experiences, you might have more difficulty adapting to challenging situations as an adult.

As Jung reminds us in *The Theory of Psychoanalysis*, sensitive children experience the world with a heightened sense of awareness and emotion that impacts their ability to cope as adults, which can often lead to depression and anxiety.

> A certain innate sensitiveness produces a special prehistory, a special way of experiencing infantile events, which in their turn are not without influence on the development of the child's view of the world. Events bound up with powerful impressions can never pass off without leaving some trace on sensitive people. Some of them remain effective throughout life, and such events can have a determining influence on a person's whole mental development.

Jung's findings were corroborated by Dr. Aron's research on the impact of negative childhood events on the highly sensitive child, as she underscores in an article for the *Journal of Jungian Theory and Practice.*

> In three different large samples, those sensitive individuals who reported relatively objective, specific negative circumstances in childhood (e.g.,

parents absent or mentally ill, alcoholism in the family, etc.) or had poorer scores on a measure of parental bonding in childhood were more depressed and anxious than were nonsensitive persons reporting similar levels of the same childhood stressors.

However, Dr. Aron discovered that highly sensitive children who didn't experience negative childhood events were no more likely to be anxious or depressed as adults than non-HSPs. In fact, because they process both positive and negative events so profoundly, highly sensitive children who were parented appropriately for their sensitivities might be *more prepared* to thrive in adulthood than nonsensitive people with a healthy childhood.

People with this gene, or with certain behaviors, such as cautiousness or physical or emotional reactivity—all signs of sensitivity—do better than others in good environments and worse than others in bad ones," says Dr. Aron in an interview by Lynn Parramore.

Parenting a Highly Sensitive Child

Looking back at the stories from my blog readers at the beginning of this chapter, it's clear how negative childhood experiences markedly shape the lives of highly sensitive adults. Certainly traumatic events can send a child on an unhappy and difficult adult trajectory. But even well-meaning parents and family members can unknowingly wound the highly sensitive child.

A parent who is not highly sensitive might have no idea why their child is so reticent, needy, or "emotional." They might push their child to be more confident, to join in with the crowd, or let things roll of his or her back, unaware how these adult expectations are impacting the sensitive child.

Even a highly sensitive parent might recognize these qualities in their child but view them as undesirable because they (the parents) were themselves berated or teased about the traits. It took me a long time to recognize my middle child's sensitive nature and that he needed more time to join in groups or leave my side. I remember with regret watching him being pulled from my car in the carpool line by his preschool teacher, crying his eyes out and begging to stay with me. I was worried he wouldn't "socialize normally" if I didn't push him to adapt. Looking back, I realize he needed more time to adjust to this new environment and a gentler separation transition.

If you are a highly sensitive person, it's quite possible one or more of your children are highly sensitive. Like me, you might worry that her sensitivities will make it harder for her to cope in an insensitive world, or that he'll be misunderstood or teased. The best thing you can do for your highly sensitive child is to fully embrace who they are and acknowledge the myriad of positive qualities your child has to offer.

Educate your children from an early age about why they react and encounter the world differently and how their unique traits afford them a richer, fuller experience of life. Many of the skills you'll learn in this book can be taught to your children as they become old enough to understand them. Let your child know that you are his or her number one advocate, and try to offer the kind of accepting, loving environment you would have wanted as a highly sensitive child.

The Wounded Child Within

If you didn't have this accepting, loving environment as a child, you've probably suffered as an adult. Because HSPs feel so deeply, the wounds of childhood are particularly debilitating and might have led you to episodes of depression, anxiety, and isolation. If you weren't allowed to express your intense emotions growing up, you might have deep wells of repressed anger or rage. Like my reader Shaleen, your youth might have left you feeling like a misfit in a world that appears insensitive and overwhelming.

If this describes your experience as an HSP, you'll likely want to see a psychotherapist at some point to help you navigate the emotions causing your suffering and to heal the childhood wounds that trigger the emotions. Therapy provides a safe and validating space to release the negative feelings you've been carrying for so long and to find healthy ways to resolve those feelings.

Ask your therapist if he or she is familiar with the term "highly sensitive person." In light of the publication of Dr. Aron's book, *The Highly Sensitive Person*, it's become a fairly mainstream concept. However, if your therapist isn't familiar with the traits, refer them to this book or to Dr. Aron's work. You want to work with a psychotherapist who understands how your innate traits have impacted your experiences and reactions to them. Be sure your therapist understands these are innate, normal personality traits—not behaviors to be cured or treated. The treatment should be for the disorders and issues that arise as a result of your sensitivities.

Remember though, you can't use the fact that you're an HSP as an excuse for your problems or a reason you can't resolve them. Although HSPs who've had troubled childhoods are more prone to depression, anxiety, and shyness, these issues certainly can be treated with therapy. HSPs with a normal childhood, and even those who experienced adult stress or trauma, are NOT more prone to these psychological problems. However, as I explain in the next chapter, high sensitivity can foster stress and overwhelm that, left unchecked, can lead to depression.

Simply understanding who you are as an HSP and that you are not weird, a misfit, or "too sensitive" is often a great start toward healing, self-acceptance, and renewed confidence. If your childhood as an HSP has impacted your joy in life, reframe your thinking about who you are and embrace your unique and beautiful qualities—and be sure to seek support to help you heal and move forward in life.

If you have a highly sensitive child, use your own childhood experiences, either positive or negative, to build a supportive and loving framework for parenting your child. Pass on a legacy of understanding, patience, and acceptance of the highly sensitive trait.

Communicate with other parents about the sensitivity trait, and share what you're learning with friends and family. When more parents and extended family understand the HSP trait, their highly sensitive children are more likely to be raised in understanding, accepting home environments, allowing them to grow into happy, confident adults.

Chapter 6: Depression, Anxiety, and Sensitivity

I'm so sensitive it doesn't take much to hurt me deeply. I deeply feel for others when they are in pain and I just "know" when someone or a group of people are upset about something. I too have been accused of being too sensitive or emotional. (All my life.) Sometimes I sit and weep for what seems like nothing to anyone else. I have been fighting depression off and on for most of my life also.

~ Marianne, reader at Live Bold and Bloom

Highly sensitive people are genetically more vulnerable to depression. As I mentioned earlier, a difficult or traumatic childhood can trigger that vulnerability in adulthood. But the characteristics of the HSP trait alone can set us up for emotional difficulties if we aren't mindful. We feel everything more intensely, and that includes the negative emotions that create stress, anxiety, and depression.

We are more motivated to think deeply about things by our strong feelings of curiosity, fear, joy, anger, etc. It's hard for us to just let things go, so we ruminate about them for a long, long time, even when we want to quiet our minds and find peace.

This internal intensity can be overwhelming, especially when it creates strong negative feelings. All of the inner reflections and anxious, critical thoughts that float around in the background of conscious thinking for the average person are more accessible, credible, and interesting to HSPs. We latch onto this detailed thinking about anxiety-producing possibilities so we can anticipate and avoid potential problems. However, we can easily become overwhelmed, creating feelings of fragility and inadequacy that foster hopelessness and depression.

Our keen sense of empathy also can be a source of depression. We feel other people's pain intensely, and we're prone to general worry and sadness about the state of world affairs and human suffering. These feelings are too much for one person to handle without absorbing and internalizing them. If an HSP lives with a depressed, highly negative, or mentally ill person or in a depressing environment, they might find they easily become depressed.

"I have always been a sensitive child, grew up in an unhappy home with an abusive, alcoholic father," says Steve, a reader on my blog. "I was bullied and rejected by my peers at school. I developed severe social anxiety in my teens which persisted to this day. I am now a 59-year-old man, disillusioned and depressed and trying to survive in an empty and meaningless life."

When you combine these emotions with the sensory overload most HSPs encounter daily, such as too much noise, bright lights, crowds, and a frantic pace of life, many of us are left feeling constantly on edge. A 2008 study about how genes affect anxiety revealed that those with a more sensitive "startle" reflex, which is found in highly sensitive people, are more genetically susceptible to anxiety disorders, making it harder for us to deal with emotional arousal.

Our nervous systems allow more stimulation to enter without automatically and unconsciously blocking it out. In addition, we turn up the volume on that stimulation by processing it in more detail than others do. What might be mildly annoying to a non-HSP is excruciatingly disturbing to the highly sensitive person.

It is this overstimulation of the mind and senses that can send us reeling into periods of anxiety and depression. Unfortunately, it isn't always possible to remove yourself from an overstimulating environment. For example, a sensitive employee might not be able to leave an overstimulating office. A sensitive child can't get up and walk out when the classroom feels overwhelming. An HSP parent cannot abandon her children when they are fraying her last nerve.

Studies have shown that when an animal believes it's unable to flee a tormenting environment, it develops feelings of "learned helplessness" and becomes hopeless and depressed, according to psychologist Martin Seligman. This is also true for humans. If you are chronically overstimulated and feel unable to control your own environment, you might be at higher risk for developing feelings of helplessness, hopelessness, and ultimately depression.

Internal body stimulation is another contributor to depression for HSPs. Because we are so tuned in to information and signals from our bodies, sensations of pain, hunger, thirst, and insufficient rest, are immediately evident to us. In fact, we can become overly concerned and worried about our health. This heightened awareness can contribute to anxiety and feelings of vulnerability that lead to depression.

Stimulation and intensity in all expressions—emotional, physical, or psychological—can cause us distress. When this distress is chronic, we become anxious and depressed. This is why it's so important for HSPs to understand their particular vulnerability to these mental illnesses and to learn skills and coping techniques to protect themselves.

According to a study published in the *Australian Journal of Psychology*, researchers found that among many strategies that help all people regulate and reduce negative emotions, HSPs tend to use certain of these strategies less.

These include the following strategies:

Accepting your feelings.

Not being ashamed of your feelings.

Believing you can cope as well as others do.

Trusting that your bad feelings will not last long.

Assuming there's hope that you can do something about your bad feelings eventually.

Part of improving your mental and emotional health is practicing these five strategies. By accepting yourself as you are without shame or judgment, with all your HSP sensitivities and emotions, you empower yourself to better cope with suffering and discomfort. You CAN cope as well as others, maybe even better than others, but you must believe you can first. And you must recognize that these negative feelings don't define you every moment of your life, for the rest of your life. You have the ability to improve your emotions.

If you didn't learn emotional coping strategies when you were young, it isn't too late to begin. Simply the awareness that you haven't been using the five strategies listed can make you feel more in control of your mental and emotional health. With awareness, you begin to notice your lack of self-trust and feelings of shame.

You can catch yourself when you notice these feelings and remind yourself of the truth. Wear a rubber band on your wrist, and when you begin ruminating about your sense of helplessness and hopelessness, gently pop the rubber band or move it to the other wrist. This creates a mental pattern interrupt, allowing you to shift gears and reframe your thinking.

Here are some additional coping strategies for HSPs dealing with anxiety and depression:

- **Manage your exposure to stimulating environments.** You know what agitates you and tires you. Too many people in the house. Too much noise. Social events that require you to be "on" for too long. In the best of times, these scenarios are depleting, but when you're depressed, they can make it more difficult to recover.

- **Practice mindfulness and meditation.** Rather than allowing your mind to dwell on past events or ruminate about future worries, train your brain to focus on the task at hand. Try to pay attention to what you're doing in the moment, even if it's a simple task like washing dishes. The practice of meditation can profoundly help your depression, as it calms your mind and allows you to disengage from the barrage of thoughts that contribute to anxiety and depressed feelings. If you'd like to learn more about mindfulness and meditation, you might enjoy my book, *Peace of Mindfulness: Everyday Rituals to Conquer Anxiety and Claim Unlimited Inner Peace.*

- **Pay extra attention to your physical health.** Don't use junk food for comfort. Eat plenty of fruits and vegetables and lean protein. If you are anxious, avoid stimulants, such as coffee, caffeinated tea, and sodas. Avoid alcohol, especially if you are depressed. Exercise moderately every day, even if it's just a short walk.

- **Create a small goal every day that you can accomplish.** Even if it's just getting the kitchen cleaned or writing a letter to someone, you will feel more in control and improve your self-esteem.

- **Intentionally focus on the positive aspects of your life.** Keep a journal in which you write down everything you're grateful for and what you are hopeful for in the future. Even if it feels false, train yourself to think positively and recognize that life has many good elements.

- **Distract yourself with fun activities that you can manage.** Watch a funny movie. Take a walk in nature with a friend. Do something creative, such as gardening or painting. Give your mind and emotions a break from the heaviness you're feeling.

- **Get plenty of rest.** If you need to nap, take a nap. Go to bed at a reasonable hour and get a good night's sleep as often as possible. If you are having trouble sleeping, go to your doctor and discuss your alternatives. Sleep is critical to feeling better.

- **Remind yourself frequently that feelings are temporary.** Even though you might believe otherwise, you won't feel depressed forever.

- **If at all possible, remove yourself from a toxic environment or relationship.** If you feel helpless, hopeless, anxious, or depressed because of a person you live with or the environment you live in, extricate yourself, even if it means finding a temporary living arrangement so you can get better. You might need the support of a close friend or therapist to help you facilitate this, especially if you don't have the energy or if you are fearful of the consequences.

Minor episodes of depression and anxiety last a few hours or days and often resolve on their own. A major depression lasts for more than two weeks, during which you feel depressed most of the time every day. The nine signs of a major depression include:

1. Feelings of sadness and a depressed mood

2. Marked loss of interest or pleasure in activities that used to give you pleasure

3. Significant weight loss or gain, or unexplained physical pain

4. Insomnia or sleeping too much

5. Feelings of either apathy or agitation

6. Loss of energy

7. Feelings of worthlessness or guilt

8. Inability to concentrate or make decisions

9. Recurrent thoughts of death or suicide

If you recognize yourself in these nine symptoms, then it's time to take action. Depression is treatable, and you should do what you can to treat it. If you are having a major depressive episode, go to your doctor or psychiatrist and to a therapist. Research confirms that the best treatment for major depression is a combination of medication and psychotherapy. Medication alone is not as effective.

Just because you are a highly sensitive person doesn't mean you will become depressed—only that you are more prone to it. Fortunately, you are also more impacted by influences that *protect* you from depression. Dr. Aron reminds us in "A Few 'Happy' Things Regarding Depression":

> Under the right conditions, your genes can make you more socially competent, resilient, and able to enjoy life than a nonsensitive person in the same environment. I think we will find that even after childhood, sensitive persons benefit more than others from a good environment (from having skilled teachers, managers at work, etc.). In a good healing environment, maybe they even heal faster from their childhood troubles than other people would.

Remember too that your sensitivity allows you to experience the positive aspects of your life more intensely and to benefit tremendously from the love, support, and encouragement of people close to you. Whatever negative repercussions might exist in being an HSP are balanced or even outweighed by the special gifts you possess.

"Only now, after having discovered and researched being a highly sensitive person, I am able to start accepting, and valuing, this rich and vibrant quality within myself," says Carrie, one of my blog readers. "I need to continue working on loving this part of myself and practicing strategies that help me cope, and thrive, in this often insensitive world."

Chapter 7: HSPs and Empaths

I am pretty sure I am an empath. One day I woke up and started to feel really sick. I had really bad chest pains , and it felt like I was having trouble breathing. Also I developed a headache and what felt like a clammy fever. This went on for a couple of hours. Anyway I ended up getting a phone call and it was my aunt. She called to tell me my dad had died of a heart attack. She said he was complaining about having chest pains, having trouble breathing, clammy fever and a really bad pounding headache. So she took him to the hospital but he ended up dying shortly after he arrived. When I found out what time he had died, I was shocked because that was around the same time all my pain and symptoms went away.

~ Mandy, reader at Live Bold and Bloom

I may meet a person once for a few minutes, and out of nowhere, at a later date, I feel their emotions thousands of miles away. I don't think or concentrate on these people. I will be in the middle of surfing the web for example, and out of nowhere I will feel their sadness or see a flash picture in my mind. I use to ignore it, but finally I started emailing or messaging these people when it happens, and I'm finding that at that time they actually are in fact sad or troubled.

~ Joe, reader at Live Bold and Bloom

Barrie Davenport

I grew up being described as a very caring, sensitive person. I knew very young that I could feel peoples' emotions and how they were feeling inside themselves. I have always found it a gift. I thank you for raising peoples' awareness so that they too can find this a gift.

~ Alena, reader at Live Bold and Bloom

If you have done any research on your own sensitive nature, you've probably come across the term "empath" somewhere along the way. The terms empath and highly sensitive person are often confused or used interchangeably. However, they aren't exactly the same.

The word empath was once used only in a science fictional context in shows such as *Star Trek*, *Charmed*, and *The Ghost Whisperer*. But now the name generally refers to people with a series of behaviors and traits that reflect a heightened ability to *feel the feelings* of other people.

Unlike empathy, which is the ability to understand and share the feelings of another, being empathic suggests you actually experience another person's emotions as your own. An empath might not be able to distinguish his own feelings from those of another person. In fact, many empaths report feeling the emotions before they cognitively understand they are feeling another person's emotions.

This reported empath trait has become mainstream enough to fill several pages on Amazon with dozens of books on the topic. In fact, during the past ten years or so, the term has become so popularized that a quick Google search turns up 640,000 results. There are entire online communities and blogs devoted to people

50

who see themselves as empaths, or who have experienced specific sensitivities and seek answers about them.

Although there isn't an established body of scientific research on the empath trait, it seems to share enough in common with the trait of elevated sensory processing sensitivity (high sensitivity) to create valid confusion. Adding to this confusion is an array of opinions about the various sensitivities that characterize empaths. So to clear up some confusion, let's start the discussion where HSPs and empaths clearly cross paths.

Most HSPs have an above-average ability to feel empathy for others. If you refer to the HSP assessment by Dr. Aron, you'll see several statements related to empathy—knowing the feelings, thoughts, and attitudes of another person.

These statements include:

- I seem to be aware of subtleties in my environment.

- Other peoples' moods affect me.

- When people are uncomfortable in a physical environment, I tend to know what needs to be done to make it more comfortable (like changing the lighting or the seating).

However, some people extend the definition of empath to include seemingly paranormal abilities to feel the feelings of other people—sometimes even when the other person isn't in the same room. Some descriptions of empaths include an ability to feel the feelings of animals, inanimate objects, and even the deceased, in addition to people.

There isn't a clinical test for empath traits as there is for the highly sensitive trait, but it appears that empath characteristics resonate with a large percentage of people, especially many HSPs.

Although not all HSPs posses all of the reported empath traits, they certainly share with empaths the heightened ability to sense the feelings of others and read their moods.

I particularly like this list of empath traits created by Elise Lebeau, PhD, who is a self-proclaimed empath and runs a blog (www.eliselebeau.com) devoted to informing and helping empaths:

Common Empath Skills

- You are unusually good at guessing how someone feels.

- You're sensitive to other peoples' moods.

- People find it easy to confide in you.

- You instinctively know what people want or need (maybe a little too much).

- You might feel someone's emotions even if they're not near you.

- You might feel other people's physical sensations in your own body.

Common Empath Side Effects

- Feeling emotionally or physically overwhelmed in crowds.

- Feeling the weight of the world on your shoulders.

- Feeling emotionally drained when you have to touch a lot of people.

- Feeling like you need to help everyone by carrying their emotional pain.

- Random mood swings (angry, sad, scared, etc.) that have nothing to do with your life events.

- Hard time falling asleep or procrastinate going to bed.

Of the twelve skills and side effects listed, I've regularly experienced ten of them myself. I haven't felt the emotions of people who aren't near me (although I sometimes have the impulse to call a friend or family member only to discover they are in distress). Nor do I literally experience the physical sensations of others. But I do soak up emotions and easily sense the moods of people who are around me. I don't view these feelings as supernatural or mystical, but more the result of my heightened empathy and emotional sensitivities as an HSP.

Having a heightened sense of empathy, whether in HSPs or empaths, is supported by some scientific research. Although "heightened empathy" isn't the same as actually feeling the feelings of someone else, this research sheds new light on the traits of empaths and why they might experience the emotions of others. New studies on mirror neurons, a small circuit of cells in the premotor cortex and inferior parietal cortex, are providing a possible explanation about why empaths are so keenly sensitive to the feelings of those around them.

Says Elise Lebeau on her blog:

> These neurons were first studied in the context of motor skills and were observed to fire up when a monkey was watching someone else perform an action. This lead to the hypothesis that watching others do something triggers an internal response that can help us mimic and imitate what we see. The very act of watching another experiencing

something activates neurons in our own brain
(Bastiaansen, Thioux and Keysers 2391–2404),
even when we are not personally performing the
action.

Marco Iacoboni, a neuroscientist at the University of California at
Los Angeles, pioneered the research on mirror neurons, the
"smart cells" in our brain that allow us to understand others.
"Empathy plays a fundamental role in our social lives," says
Iacoboni. "It allows us to share emotions, experiences, needs, and
goals. Not surprisingly, there is much empirical evidence
suggesting a strong link between mirror neurons (or some general
forms of neuronal mirroring) and empathy."

In his book *Mirroring People*, Iacoboni introduces these neurons
as the potential seat of empathy and morality, because they seem
to be involved in how we can perceive and interpret the
experiences of other people. These neurons are triggered by
observing a physical gesture in another person, which then fires
the same physiological neurons in the observer.

"In short, mirror neurons allow us to create a very specific,
contextual internal representation of what others are experiencing
by firing our own brain cells to bring meaning and understanding
to the actions of others," says Elise Lebeau.

Although mirror neurons afford a sophisticated cognitive method
of understanding the feelings of others and putting those into a
particular context, science has not yet bridged the divide between
heightened empathy and actually feeling another person's
feelings. Is there a biological apparatus that allows empaths to
experience the emotions of others, even of those thousands of
miles away? Perhaps another study provides a clue.

University College London cognitive neuroscientist Sarah-Jayne Blakemore discovered a condition known as mirror-touch synesthesia. This condition occurs in hyper-empathetic people who actually sense they're being touched when they witness others being touched. Or they feel pain when observing someone in pain.

Think about a time when you watched someone bump their head or burn their hand picking up a hot pan. As you observed them in pain, you probably winced at the thought of their pain and what it must feel like. We all empathize to an extent with the physical feelings of others, but for a person with mirror-touch synesthesia, they don't just wince at the thought of pain—they actually feel it. For these people, the area of the brain that creates this empathy is hyperactive.

The researchers in the University College London study had the mirror-touch synesthetes complete a questionnaire designed to measure empathy. For example, they were asked to agree or disagree with statements including, "I can tune into how someone feels rapidly and intuitively." The mirror-touch synesthetes scored significantly higher than people without synesthesia.

For our discussion on empaths, perhaps it would have been more telling had the question been, "I can rapidly and intuitively *feel* how someone feels." But it's not a far leap to wonder if some people are able to feel the physical sensations of others, why shouldn't they be able to feel their feelings?

The purpose of this book isn't to prove or disprove whether or not empath traits are legitimate. The lines get blurry between being highly empathetic to another's emotions (so much so that you begin to feel the same way) and actually feeling the feelings of someone who might or might not be in the same room with you.

You might be a highly sensitive person who literally feels the feelings of other people, and you might even feel responsible for taking away the other person's pain. Or, like me, you might be a highly sensitive person who easily picks up on the emotions of others and is strongly affected by them.

For the HSP who isn't an empath, the cues for sensitivity to emotion are external (like a facial expression or body language). The empath experiences the feelings first, then later has thoughts about them. This distinction can cause empaths a great deal of confusion, as it's difficult to sort their own emotions from those of others. In fact, many empaths encounter tremendous distress and suffering as a result of their abilities.

"I have often felt as though something was wrong with me. I feel as though I read people and what they are thinking in almost any given situation," says my reader, Buffy. "Because of this, it causes me huge social anxiety. I have made many poor choices in my life, and I carry my head in shame, making it very hard to face my family. I also have to deal with post-traumatic stress from all of this. I'm crying as I'm posting this."

Perhaps the most difficult aspect of being an empath (or an HSP with strong empathic skills) is not knowing why you have these abilities and how to manage them. The sheer volume of information and feelings you experience from others is overwhelming. Couple that with anxiety about why you experience these feelings, and you create a perfect storm for depression and unhealthy coping reactions.

However, you can manage the barrage of input and protect yourself from overwhelm with a few strategies:

- Learn how to dial back on outside input by focusing more on your own thoughts and activities. When you notice yourself picking up on the feelings around you, get busy doing something that distracts you and occupies your mind. You don't have to absorb everything that comes into your field of emotional sensitivity.

- When you are in crowds of people, imagine or visualize yourself surrounded by a protective shield that blocks the negative energy floating around you. If you begin to sense someone's negative emotions, imagine the feelings bouncing off your protective shield, unable to touch you.

- With family and friends, your desire to respond to their emotions and help them can be overwhelming. You sense something is wrong, and you feel responsible for correcting it. However, these people might not want your help or haven't tuned in to their own emotions yet. Give yourself permission to let go of responsibility, and affirm in your mind (or out loud) that they are responsible for their own well-being.

- Spend plenty of time on your own in a quiet environment, away from family and friends. This gives you time to recharge and calm your emotions.

- It is particularly important to let go of responsibility in romantic relationships where you feel so tied to the other person and their well-being. If you become too entangled in your partner's emotions, you'll have a hard time distinguishing between theirs and your own. Also, be aware that you might not always read your partner's emotions correctly.

- Allowing your partner to process his or her emotions alone (and then come to you later if they wish) is often a better strategy for the health of your relationship in the long run. This allows them to fully experience and identify what they are feeling before you unravel it for them, which can cause resentment or confusion. Most people are perfectly capable of figuring out their own "stuff" given time. If not, they probably don't want to figure it out.

- Others will notice your ability to solve their problems and understand their pain, and some people will take advantage of your time and energy as a result. Create boundaries with others when you notice you're feeling overwhelmed or drained. Learn to say "no" and to create limits on your willingness to help, even when you want to be always available. Your emotional health is too important.

- Avoid trolling for people with problems to solve. Your nature makes you inclined to want to help, and if someone doesn't come to you, you might feel the need to seek them out. You don't need to ask for problems that aren't yours. Save your energy for those who are close to you and for a time when they really need you.

One of the main difficulties empaths experience is not feeling safe and secure in their environment. With so many negative emotions swirling around them, they are often hypervigilant, always expecting the next wave of unpleasant emotions to sweep over them. This hypervigilance alone creates anxiety and distress, because it's so hard to simply relax into life and enjoy the moment. Sometimes empaths pull back altogether from engaging with people simply to avoid the emotional stimulation. Isolating yourself can be as destructive to your psyche as becoming overstimulated.

Take notice if you think you are pulling back from people, and take small steps toward reintegrating yourself with others. In fact, you might start by connecting with other empaths. There are a variety of online communities for support, such as Elise Lebeau's online forum (http://empathcommunity.eliselebeau.com/) and this Google Group (https://groups.google.com/forum/#!forum/empath).

It's impossible for anyone, even empaths, to control the emotions of others or anything that happens in the world around them. The *only* thing we can control is ourselves and how we choose to respond. Easier said than done, I know, but with awareness and practice, empaths *can* feel safe and able to "let go" of the dread that comes with the empathic territory. By accepting who you are and recognizing that your empath gift is yours to control and manage, you can live comfortably and happily. Remember, you are in charge of this gift—not the other way around.

If you see yourself as an empath, in addition to being highly sensitive, it's comforting to know what's happening, how to manage it, and that others share these same traits. Hopefully science will one day have a better explanation for the biology of this unique gift, but in the meantime, if you'd like to learn more about the empath experience, I find Elise Lebeau's blog (www.eliselebeau.com) to be balanced and practical, with a variety of useful resources and support for especially for empaths.

Chapter 8: The Power of Friendships

Not too long ago, I was talking to a friend about another close friend who had stopped contacting me or initiating time together. This close friend was going through a personal crisis, one that I'd been through myself, so I couldn't understand why she'd backed off when I could have been a support to her. We'd always been close, talking nearly every day, so her behavior was particularly confusing and painful.

The friend I shared this news with had an immediate answer to my dilemma. "You're too good at reading people," she said. "I always know if I want the truth, I'll come to you. If I'm not ready to face or share the truth, then I'd probably avoid you too." As a highly sensitive person, I should have figured this out on my own, but my sensitivities were still stuck in what felt like a rejection.

It's been a difficult lesson accepting that my ability to "see" people and read what they're thinking and feeling isn't always appreciated or valued. It can feel too intense and vulnerable for some people, especially for those who don't want to reveal much about themselves. Non-HSPs in particular are often baffled by questions like, "What's going on? I can tell something's off with you today." It feels like an invasion to them—like I've been secretly watching them get undressed.

As an HSP, you might be confused by your non-HSP friends' ability to let things roll off their shoulders or their seeming lack of sensitivity to your feelings about something important to you. You might wonder why they don't reciprocate the same level of interest and intensity in the friendship or respond to your needs the same way you respond to theirs. You might also question why they remain happy with small talk about kids, sports, or gossip when you'd much rather discuss beefier topics, like say, the meaning of life or world peace. Our need for depth and intense connection can be off-putting or intimidating to those who prefer a lighter interaction.

You might find friendships fall away as a result of a non-HSP friend simply getting overwhelmed with your intensity. Conversely, you might have dropped a friend because you found them too boring or superficial over time. Your non-HSP friends might have been intrigued by you and your sensitive nature upon first meeting you. They probably found your personality unique and interesting, but over time the novelty wears off, and they want to go back to what they consider a "normal" interaction that doesn't involve so much intensity. If you can't lighten up, they drift away.

Here's what one of my blog readers says about having friendships as an HSP:

> I love to care for people around me, friends, family, strangers. I put so much of time, energy, love and patience into every friend, not because I have to, but I want to and cannot avoid it. However, I am misunderstood to be more dramatic, crazy, weird. I let my friends leave when they want to, even though I want them to stop and be with me. I never ask them because I feel I caused them a lot of pain in having to deal with me. I feel I am responsible for having the people I love abandon me. I feel like an orphan quite often. Words hurt me really bad. Not

every friend can understand, and I do not expect
them to. But I end up losing people whom I love
and care for.

Of course, an HSP will take the loss of a friendship really hard. You might feel betrayed or taken advantage of by a close friend who has decided to back off from you. You might experience deep grief with the loss and worry that you aren't capable of holding on to friends. With too many of these experiences, you might begin to isolate yourself or hold back from friendships because you don't know whether or not you can trust a new friend to stick by you.

This doesn't have to be the case, especially when you discern how to choose friends and how to manage the non-HSP friendships you value. On the positive side, HSPs make excellent friends to those who appreciate them and accept their sensitive qualities. Because they are highly empathetic and tuned in to the feelings of others, HSPs are often there for their friends even before the friends realize they are in need. An HSP might say something to a friend like, "You seemed distressed," and it isn't until this remark is made that the other person apprehends they actually *are* distressed.

Lily, an HSP reader on my blog, says, "I am very good with people. I pick up on their emotions before they do. As a result, I find it very easy to make friends. I see it as a gift." When you view your HSP traits as a gift, you learn how and when to offer your gift to your friends and which friends truly value the skills you have to offer.

Empath Friendships

Lily's strong empathic skills have allowed her to make new connections and nurture her friendships. However, true empaths might find their ability to feel the emotions of their friends more of a drain than a gift. An empath might attract many friends because of their ability to read and feel emotions. But an empath should be extremely discerning about who they embrace as a close friend and how particular groups of friends can impact them.

Even the best of friends can easily infect you with their bad temper or unhappiness. Some friends might unknowingly become "energy vampires" who deplete your energy. Because empaths are such devoted friends, they might not feel comfortable backing off when they should for their own emotional well-being. Empaths very much want their friendships to be warm, intimate, and bonded, but it's easy for them to fall into the rescuer role and allow friends to overwhelm and deplete them. "I do not seek out friendships actively, but people seem to pop up in my life and usually it's for me to help in some way," says my empath reader, Jennifer.

As an empath, you might have certain friendships that work well one-on-one, but when you add another friend or a group of friends to the mix, the dynamic shifts, and you might feel drained, left out, or even bullied. It is up to you to protect yourself from toxic friendships or interactions that cause you suffering and exhaustion. "I had a friend tell me once that I seek out the broken people, the people that sap me of all that is me," says my blog reader, Erin. "I don't do this on purpose, because honestly who the heck wants to be fatigued all the time or have stomachaches?"

You would be wise to tell your close friends about your empath traits and how they can support you. But even caring friends aren't always aware of how their behavior or moods can impact you. Nor can you expect your friends to manage all their own feelings and actions to accommodate you. This is a relationship dance you and your friends can navigate with open and honest communication and respect. Friendships are vital to the happiness of sensitive, empathic people, so it is well worth the effort to choose friends carefully and nurture them with patience and love.

The Helper Sensitive

One of the most valuable gifts of sensitive people is their ability to be great listeners who can get to the meat of an issue more quickly than most. Because of these skills, HSPs make their friends feel supported, loved, and truly heard. In fact, HSPs are genuinely interested in helping their friends and family members solve problems and overcome challenges. As an HSP, you might find that people who "need fixing" tend to gravitate toward you because they see someone willing to listen to their troubles and serve as a freelance therapist.

This dynamic can become one-sided, and you might begin to feel the relationship isn't reciprocal or enjoyable. This situation is one in which HSPs can run into trouble because they are so reticent to give up on a friendship. "HSPs are also such good observers that they can usually see when there's something troubling a friend or there is something wrong between the two of them. They take criticism seriously and try to change their behavior to suit their friend," reminds Dr. Aron in a November 2008 blog. Clarifying boundaries in your friendships is more important for HSPs who tend to accommodate others beyond what's appropriate.

As an HSP, you pick up on subtleties in the environment, and therefore you notice things your friends might not perceive. As a result, you have access to more information and can offer a broader, more in-depth perspective on situations or challenges. Your powerful intuition has likely served your friends well, as you might sense danger or a notice a negative environment when others don't pick up on it. Your gut instinct gives you keen insights and awareness that your long-time friends have likely noticed about you over time and have come to appreciate.

Because you're so mindful and attentive to others, you go out of your way to make it easy for your friends. You're likely the person who coordinates getting together or notices when someone in the group is feeling left out. You make a point of introducing like-minded friends you think would be a good match. Even in public and with strangers, you might be the person who steps out of the way on the sidewalk to let someone pass or makes room on the elevator when it's crowded.

A good two-thirds of HSPs are introverts, and if that's you, you might find you prefer small groups of friends, or just one or two best friends with whom you spend your time, have deep conversations, and share your problems. Introverted HSPs need to be selective in choosing their few close friends and communicative about their unique HSP gifts and sensitivities, especially with non-HSPs. An extraverted non-HSP can be a wonderful friend for an introverted HSP, as long as the two understand and respect the different ways you experience the world. A warm and talkative extraverted friend can help an introverted HSP feel accepted and liked.

Extraverts make up about one-third of the HSP population, and these sensitive extraverts enjoy larger groups of friends, family gatherings, and meeting new people. However, unlike other extraverts, highly sensitive extraverts need time alone to recharge after group events or a lot of social stimulation.

The combination of extraversion and sensitivity makes for great leadership qualities and attracts a lot of people to you, but you still can get your feelings hurt easily if a group sees you as too unusual or sensitive. As an extravert, you can generally find another group whose dynamic is more suited to your nature if you begin to feel unappreciated. During challenging times like these, an extraverted HSP might wish to turn to an introverted HSP friend who will carefully listen and offer thoughtful advice.

In your friendships, remember these strategies to build healthy, mutually satisfying connections that last:

- Communicate with your non-HSP friends about the HSP trait and characteristics if they don't know about them. Tell them about your specific sensitivities and how you tend to respond to the world and other people. Be sure to let friends know that your desire to spend time alone does not mean that you no longer like them.

- Define exactly what friendship means to you—how you want to be a friend and how you want others to be a friend to you. Remember, friendship is a two-way street, and you can't allow your sensitivity needs to dominate the connection.

- Don't always assume comments or behaviors from your non-HSP friends are insensitive or uncaring. Their intentions might be perfectly fine, but your interpretation can be skewed by your nature. Communication is key to understanding one another.

- Be mindful of your own intensity and how it affects others, especially non-HSP friends you truly value. If you sense it can be too much for them, learn to temper the intensity to keep the friendship balanced.

- If you are an introverted HSP, look for friends who share your quiet and thoughtful nature, and for those who are accepting and kind. Use your keen intuition to discern the demeanor and inner nature of a potential friend.

- If you're an extraverted HSP, look for friends as creative and passionate about things as you are. Join groups where you're likely to find an atmosphere of acceptance.

- Pay attention to friends who constantly turn to you for support during difficulties, so they don't overwhelm you with their needs. Learn to set boundaries with these friends, and ask them to reciprocate more often.

- Allow yourself to let go of friends who cause you more pain and conflict than joy. You don't have to be responsible for maintaining every friendship.

- As an HSP, your first step toward better friendships is releasing societal and family expectations about friendships. Don't worry about the number of friends you "should" have. Instead figure out what "being friends" with someone means to you. Remember, it's really OK to be selective.

A mind set I've embraced as an HSP is understanding that every friendship doesn't have to be the same. There are people in my life who are my deep-thinking, more intense friends. I have friends who I know would be there for me in an instant if I needed them, and others I couldn't count on for that help—but they are still a lot of fun to be around. There are those who are great for a dinner out and light conversation and those who make me laugh for hours.

Every friendship has a unique dynamic and enriches my life in a profound and wonderful way. Yes, there have been friendships I've lost along the way. There have been occasions of misunderstandings and hurt feelings. But as I've learned to accept myself more as an HSP and recognize that all people aren't wired the same way, I've come to have more understanding for those who view the world differently from me.

As a final note on friendship, the most important thing to remember as an HSP is this: be yourself. We HSPs work so hard to fit in, to ensure everyone likes us, to take care of our friends, and help others with their problems. Sometimes in our efforts, we lose ourselves. We forget that it's OK to be who we are, sensitivities and all, so we pretend or stuff our feelings. The best friends are those who are authentic, and those who are your *real* friends will love you for exactly who you are.

Chapter 9: HSPs and Love Relationships

HSPs are extraordinary people, and they can make extraordinary love partners. Because they are sensitive, caring, and intuitive, they willingly offer these amazing gifts to the one they love. If these gifts are accepted with appreciation, and if they are reciprocated (even to a small extent), the relationship can thrive on a deeply intimate and joyful level.

Your conscientiousness, truthful nature, and concern for your loved one's welfare make you a highly reliable, caring partner. You are deeply committed to your relationship and to working things out, especially because breaking up is extremely difficult for you. In an intimate, love relationship, you're adept at picking up on nonverbal cues and knowing what your partner is feeling, often before he or she does. You recognize what is deep and spiritual about your partner, which makes the relationship even more intimate.

As a highly sensitive person, you might find an ideal relationship with another HSP. Because you are both so tuned into one another, you are able to resolve conflict before it bubbles over into anger and resentment, emotions that are extremely uncomfortable for you to tolerate. You are both caring and sensitive to the other's needs, and you likely want to please each other.

In my own relationship with another HSP, we laugh at how often we check in with each other to ensure everything is OK, and how we try to anticipate the other's needs. We both enjoy quiet time together, socializing in small groups of close friends, and staying away from crowded, loud spaces. We both seek depth and meaning in the relationship and spend a lot time talking about topics that are substantial and engaging. However, since we are both introverts, we have to be proactive about socializing and stretching outside of the comfort of our close relationship.

"Boredom is a special problem for a pair of similars, two HSPs in particular," reminds Dr. Aron in her blog on "The Highly Sensitive Person in Love." "They may be initially excited to find their similarities, but in time tend to use each other as a sanctuary rather than as a partner in exploring new experiences."

If you are an introverted HSP, an extraverted HSP might be a good match for you. While they enjoy more social activities than you, extraverted HSPs feel things deeply just like you. The sensory stimulation they encounter in social settings also can overwhelm them, despite their desire to participate. This is where you can balance the extraverted HSP, and he or she can balance you.

HSP extraverts can find compassion and understanding in a highly sensitive introvert. The introverted partner can help the extraverted HSP pull back from the socializing they crave in order to recharge and avoid overstimulation. Introverts can be encouraged to stretch themselves into new situations that are uncomfortable at first, but with their HSP partner they feel safe to explore.

When two HSPs find each other and fall in love, the relationship can be transformative, particularly if both partners are self-aware and understand the unique needs of being highly sensitive. However, the odds of an HSP finding and choosing another HSP as a partner are relatively small. HSPs make up just 15 to 20 percent of the population, so it's far more likely you'll connect with a non-HSP love interest. If you're specifically looking for an extraverted HSP, your chances are much slimmer, as they make up just 30 percent of all HSPs.

These odds don't mean you are doomed to a bad relationship. HSPs and non-HSPs can have wonderful, satisfying, and deeply loving relationships. But it does require communication, patience, and mutual understanding by both partners. As an HSP, your job in seeking a life partner is to find someone who has strong emotional intelligence and self-awareness—and someone who has a desire to understand you and love you *because* of your unique gifts, not *despite* them.

Says my reader, Aaron, about his HSP wife, "My wife has been called shy, and others mistake this for a weakness. I tend to think that there are very few genuine weaknesses, only misapplied strengths." He chooses to see his wife's so-called shyness as a strength. This is the kind of enlightened partner an HSP needs and deserves.

Highly sensitive people long for a supportive, loving partner, whether it's another HSP or not. Says Dr. Aron in an article by Amy Scholten, MPH,

> Relationships are extremely important for well-being, especially the well-being of highly sensitive people. One of the main reasons for this is that, as a whole, highly sensitive people tend to have lower self-esteem than the rest of the population. Close

relationships can offer us support, and the chance
to experience our sensitivity as valuable.

Since HSPs tend to struggle with feeling accepted in a less-than-sensitive world, they also often have problems with self-acceptance.

Unfortunately, this makes them more prone to choosing the wrong partner, fearing they can't find anyone better. Says Kate, one of my blog commenters, "I have often attracted abusive relationships and narcissists. I have learned to spot them and ensure I am not in those kind of relationships at all because they do know how to manipulate you. I thought this was a curse."

As HSPs, our sensitive, caring natures make us prime candidates for romantic partners who carry a lot of emotional baggage. We can easily get sucked into the vortex of their needs and issues, too afraid to break away and face the discomfort of ending a relationship.

HSPs who don't value or understand their own traits might gravitate toward the type of person they think they *should* be themselves—one who is extraverted, highly confident, and not overly sensitive. We choose these mates to balance us and make up for what we feel we lack. Or we become attracted to qualities in a partner that seem exciting and different at first, but over time the qualities become extremely annoying or overwhelming.

Sometimes this confusion is simply the result of an HSP suddenly feeling overwhelmed and overstimulated in the relationship and not understanding his or her own need to pull back. "Why do I constantly question the happy, healthy relationship I am in with my boyfriend of two years?" asks my reader, Kaitlyn. "I love him so much, but yet, I am constantly asking myself if he is right for me, and wondering if I would feel free or relieved if I left him, even though he is near and dear to me."

Dealing with Conflict

At some point, conflict and misunderstanding will inevitably arise between highly sensitive and less sensitive partners. Fortunately, most of these difficulties are not insurmountable when the non-HSP partner is motivated to understand the sensitivities of his or her spouse and when the HSP openly communicates his or her traits and needs. The very nature of a love relationship requires open communication, intimacy and vulnerability in order to survive. Intimacy is the ability to be close, to be authentic, and to feel safe as you reveal yourself to another. You cannot have this kind of intimacy without acceptance, understanding, and kindness toward each other.

However, real problems occur in a relationship when HSPs and non-HSPs view intimacy and vulnerability differently, and one or the other isn't motivated by kindness and the desire to understand the other. To the non-HSP, his highly sensitive spouse might appear needy, insecure, intense, and picky. The HSP partner might view her significant other as shallow, insensitive, unconscious, and brash. Communication shuts down as each person feels misunderstood and defensive.

As an HSP, you might feel the pain of the relationship disconnect more profoundly than your spouse. Arguments, unkind comments, the silent treatment, and passive aggressive comments feel like daggers in your heart. Where your partner might get over a conflict quickly and let it roll off her back, you probably dwell on it for days, wondering what it all means and whether or not it spells doom to your relationship.

"So now the big problem is that I'm married to a man who is a good person but is passive aggressive," says my reader, Marsha. "He 'uses' his moods and emotions to get his way and to keep me in line with his emotional comfort zone. He has only to 'go silent' for a short time and I'm all over myself acting out my childhood again, still trying to 'get Daddy in a good humor.' How can I learn to be less aware of his moods and less reactive to them? It's a form of bullying—it's emotional bullying."

It might well be emotional bullying by Marsha's spouse, or it could be that Marsha is keenly aware of any mood shifts that reflect her father's former behavior when she was a child. Marsha's husband might be completely unaware of how his moods or behaviors are impacting her. Or he might have figured out her Achilles heel and is taking full advantage of it.

It's easy for both partners in an HSP/non-HSP relationship to slip into a pattern unconsciously in which the non-HSP uses moods and words to subtly manipulate the HSP. The more sensitive partner, sensing his or her spouse's unhappiness or shift in mood, will quickly accommodate in order to smooth things over. Over time, even the most well-meaning spouse will figure out it doesn't take much to get his or her way.

As an HSP, the responsibility is yours to thoroughly and openly communicate with your partner not only what this trait is, but also exactly how your sensitivities impact your needs and behavior. You can't expect a non-HSP romantic partner to understand you if they have never heard of the highly sensitive trait or if they have a misconception about it.

By the same token, you'll need to meet your partner in the middle at times and give her some grace related to her perceived insensitivities. If you know your spouse is loving in general and doesn't want to hurt you, there's no need to call him on the carpet every time he speaks too loudly or makes a remark that causes you to bristle. Pick your battles, and learn to take care of your own emotional needs, as you can't expect any one person to meet all your needs or read your mind in every situation.

If you are in a relationship that isn't working, one in which your HSP spouse or partner doesn't appreciate your gifts or handle your sensitivities with dignity and love, then the toxicity of the relationship will certainly drive one or both of you to leave. More than likely, you'll be the one hanging on in despair, hoping beyond hope that things will get better because you can't bear to cut the cord. In time, you might become withdrawn and depressed, as you feel more and more overwhelmed by your need to "fix" things or accept far less than you need from the other person.

Says my reader, Jennifer, "I'm married to a very unaffectionate man whom I can't get a general hug from and feel as though I have failure to thrive sometimes. I wear my heart openly, and when I feel as though it's not reciprocated, I hurt inside deeply." This failure to thrive is a huge red flag that your relationship is in trouble. Your love relationship should be a safe haven where you feel lifted up rather than dragged down.

If this isn't the case for you, then it's probably past time to take stock of your relationship to determine whether or not it can be salvaged. Here are some signs of a toxic relationship that should be a warning for you:

- You find yourself walking on eggshells all the time for fear you'll upset your partner.

- Your needs and desires are always pushed aside. It's always about the other person's needs first and foremost.

- Your spouse disregards your sensitivities and even makes fun of them, calls you names, or puts you down about them.

- You don't feel comfortable expressing your ideas or thoughts openly.

- Your partner takes advantage of you and expects you to do all the emotional work.

- You frequently find yourself in the role of therapist or parent to your spouse rather than equal, adult partners.

- You compromise your own values, traditions, friendships, and needs in order to maintain the relationship.

- Your partner regularly ignores your requests to speak more softly, turn down the TV, stop wearing perfume or cologne, or to support you with any of your sensitivities. She thinks you are wrong, and she has every right to do as she pleases.

- Your partner withholds affection or makes you uncomfortable physically or sexually.

- You're more often fatigued, physically distressed, or drained around your partner than not.

- You simply don't feel loved, respected, or appreciated.

Despite being fearful or worried about rocking the boat, you must communicate your concerns to your spouse and ask him or her to work on the issues in counseling together. A good therapist who is familiar with highly sensitive traits can help your partner understand you, and help both of you create boundaries and communication skills. This step could save your relationship and prevent you both from experiencing further pain and disconnection.

However, if your desire to resolve conflicts and improve the relationship is not appreciated or reciprocated, you should see this as another red flag. You cannot carry the burden of an unhealthy relationship alone and expect things to get better. It's time to consider leaving the relationship before it completely breaks you.

Getting the Love You Need

One of the more positive traits of HSPs is the tendency to be an idealist. You want to find the "one." You deeply desire to have an intimate, connected relationship. You believe in working hard to constantly improve your relationship. You crave peace and calm between you and your loved one. Most relationships require effort and attention, and for an HSP, it might require a bit more effort than the norm to achieve your vision—but the payoff can be profoundly rewarding for an aware, dedicated couple willing to do the work and to see the best in each other.

A loving, happy, satisfying relationship is completely possible, whether you are with another HSP or non-HSP. If you are both motivated to make it work and have a foundation of love and mutual respect, you can find a way to navigate your differences. As you endeavor to find a relationship or to improve the one you have, here are some strategies to keep in mind:

- If you are searching for love, look for someone who is emotionally mature, self-aware, and open to learning about who you are. Run as fast as you can from narcissists, difficult people, and those with a lot of emotional baggage who will drain you.

- Keep your eyes open for other HSPs with whom you might connect. Now that you know the traits for yourself, they will be easier for you to spot in others. If you use a online dating site or service, mention your HSP trait in your profile. It might help screen out those you don't want and attract those you do.

- Remember, the key to finding the love you want is loving yourself first. Now that you know your traits aren't "issues" or mental problems, you can view them as amazing gifts you can offer a lucky partner. Embrace your gifts and love yourself all the more for them.

- Communicate openly and often about your sensitive traits. The key to success in any relationship is communication, but it's particularly important in this situation where your partner might not know about HSPs or understand that the traits are normal. Share this book or Dr. Aron's book with your partner.

- Ask for what you need and set boundaries. This is also part of communication. If you feel overwhelmed by noise, ask your spouse to move it to another room. If you need to spend some time alone, let your partner know you love him, but you need a break for an hour or so. This goes both ways, so remember, you might need to compromise at times—as long as neither of you are compromising core values or your sense of self.

- Catch yourself when pleasing or compromising for the sake of keeping the peace. You might feel uncomfortable with conflict, but you must stand up for yourself. Don't allow fear or discomfort to keep you from doing what is best for you.

- Whether you're a woman or man, never feel you must cover up your sensitive nature in order to accommodate your partner or anyone else. Be yourself and ask your spouse to accept you for who you are.

- If you find confrontation and conflict too arousing or uncomfortable, seek the help of a trained therapist to help you and your spouse. By avoiding conflict resolution, you are setting yourself up for trouble. Take action if you want to save your relationship.

In general, it's important to work on your own confidence and self-esteem issues so that you can offer your best self to your partner. The more confident you are in yourself, the more pride you will have in your unique traits, which will make you a more interesting, attractive partner. You can rebuild confidence with practice and persistence, by working to change self-defeating thoughts and behaviors. (Check out my program on building confidence—http://simpleselfconfidence.com/—or my confidence books—see my Amazon author page at www.barriedavenport/author.com —if you need support with this.)

Thoughts for Highly Sensitive Men

Confidence can be a real problem for HSPs in relationships, as our culture reinforces that we are less desirable partners. This is particularly true for males who are highly sensitive—half of the HSP population. Males in our culture are supposed to be strong, competitive, and less sensitive. Most young boys are raised to understand a sensitive man is not a "real man." A highly sensitive man (HSM) might grow up feeling inferior in his manhood because he doesn't fit the traditional gender stereotype. If a sensitive boy had a father who adamantly reinforced this stereotype, the feelings of inferiority are even more pronounced.

Barrie Davenport

Learning that the sensitivity traits are perfectly normal for both women and men is the beginning of self-acceptance for many HSMs. Rick Belden, author of the book, *Iron Man Family Outing: Poems about Transition into a More Conscious Manhood*, describes his feelings about recognizing himself as a highly sensitive man in an article for The Good Men Project:

> For the first time, someone was telling me that I could be not just merely sensitive, but *highly* sensitive, and still be a man. This was a possibility that had never been presented to me before, not in person and certainly not in the culture at large, and it was the first step in beginning to own my sensitivity, not just as a valuable element but a *defining* element of my masculine identity.

In heterosexual romantic relationships, a highly sensitive man might assume that women desire only this stereotypical male partner, an assumption that has some basis in reality. Because many HSMs want so desperately to fit the stereotype, they can find themselves in confusing and painful relationships with women who send mixed messages about how they want a man to behave. A woman might initially respond positively to your sensitive nature, only to become bored later, wanting someone more "exciting" and "manly." You might have great friendships with women and become interested in them romantically, only to be rejected when you express this interest.

HSMs can unconsciously protect themselves from rejection by behaving in ways that push women away or by avoiding emotional intimacy. Or an HSM might purposely seek out women who want a more assertive, dominant partner, even though that's not the HSM's nature. It's particularly difficult for men who've spent years (decades) pretending to be something other than who they really are to accept and embrace their sensitive natures and to attract women who also recognize and appreciate their sensitivities.

Interesting research from The Face Research Lab at the University of Glasgow in Scotland (www.faceresearch.org) suggests that many women do prefer a more sensitive *looking* man. Women were asked to look at pairs of faces of the same man but with subtle differences making one appear more masculine and the other having softer features.

Researchers were able to predict how masculine a woman prefers her men based on statistics for mortality rates, life expectancy, and the impact of communicable disease for her country. The women from the healthiest countries had a clear preference for men with more feminine, sensitive features. Women from the unhealthy countries chose the masculine faces, apparently because more testosterone indicates a healthier, more virile man.

What does this mean for the highly sensitive man and his relationship success? Perhaps nothing, as you will likely find that a discerning, sensitive woman is more likely to select a partner based on internal qualities rather than external features alone. Finding this type of woman certainly narrows the field, but holding out for the right partner is well worth the wait.

If you are a highly sensitive man, or you think you might be, it is critical for the health of your love relationships, and also for your mental health, that you embrace who you are and allow your sensitive nature to be fully expressed. If you've been pretending to be the tough, aggressive stereotypical male and disowning your sensitive side, you are living half a life. Denying who you are and repressing your emotions can lead to serious mental health issues, such as isolation, anxiety, and depression.

Having the courage to be yourself is actually the bravest, most evolved endeavor you'll ever undertake. I love what Rick Belden says about real masculinity when he reminds that

> Sensitivity is not the absence of toughness, but is, in many ways, the very *embodiment* of toughness. It takes a great deal of inner strength and resiliency to maintain your sensitivity in a world that seems to go out of its way to beat it out of you, often literally. If that's not a demonstration of strength, courage, and resolve consistent with any reasonable definition of masculinity, I don't know what is.

The key to happy relationships for the HSM is being true to yourself, defining exactly what YOU want in a relationship, and then seeking a partner who can offer you that. In fact, highly sensitive men have so much to offer in healthy, mature romantic relationships.

Says Ted Zeff, PhD and author of *The Highly Sensitive Person's Survival Guide*, in an article on "Healing the Highly Sensitive Male":

> The highly sensitive male may have trouble fitting into the narrow mold of a stereotypical male, but he has many wonderful qualities. Some of these include:
>
> Compassion
>
> Gentleness
>
> The ability to act as a peacemaker
>
> Concern about the humane treatment of animals

Finely Tuned

A sense of responsibility

Conscientiousness

Creativity

The tendency to feel love deeply

A great intuitive ability

An awareness of their unity with all beings

The ability to have and appreciate deep spiritual experiences

A woman of depth, substance, compassion, creativity, and sensitivity will find these qualities highly desirable. If you are in a relationship with a woman who doesn't know about or understand your sensitive nature, give her the benefit of the doubt that she'll respond positively if you communicate with her about it.

Even if you still have an uneasy relationship with your sensitivities, your love relationship can be the safe haven where you express who you are without shame, judgment, or fear of rejection. With the support of the woman you love, you'll begin to see your highly sensitive nature as an asset rather than a weakness.

Chapter 10: HSPs and Empaths at Work

My first job after graduating from college was working as an assistant in the public relations and special events office of a major department store in Atlanta, Georgia. I wasn't much more than a glorified secretary in the beginning, but the nature of the work required I regularly interact with senior management.

Having graduated with a degree in English literature from a liberal arts university, I was ill-prepared for working in a corporate environment. But I was even less prepared for the demeanor and management style of many of the leaders in the organization.

Many of the men and some of the women managed by fear and intimidation—yelling, cursing, and barking demands at the staff. Most of my coworkers took it in stride, but I found it extremely disconcerting, especially if the behavior were directed toward me. When I complained about it to my associates, I was told to get a thicker skin and accept that "this is the way it's done in retail." If I didn't like it, I should leave.

One of my bosses in particular seemed to take pleasure in pulling her staff members into a conference room and verbally ripping them to shreds. She wasn't satisfied if you didn't leave crying and humiliated. After a few years in this environment, I was so anxious and unhappy, I left to work at another corporate retailer, but one that included (and practiced) "The Golden Rule" as part of their mission statement. I was also able to work in a private office rather than the shared and noisy cubicle space I previously had. This was a much better fit for a highly sensitive person who thrived in an environment of mutual respect, calm, and professionalism.

Even so, many of the qualities I brought to the table as a highly sensitive person weren't viewed as essential skills in most of my work environments through the years. Being assertive, driven, and productive were far more valuable traits than having empathy, using interpersonal skills, or picking up on subtleties in the environment. Of course, I learned to compensate for my sensitive personality and tried hard to fit in with the professional culture and expectations of whatever organization I worked for. This often took a toll on my energy and emotional well-being, but at the time, I simply didn't realize I had a choice. I thought work was supposed to be stressful and exhausting.

There's no question, it can be extremely difficult for sensitive employees to cope at work, much less thrive and feel happy. "I feel lost at times because others I'm around in my welding work area aren't the same as me," says one of my HSP blog readers about his job. "I try to fit in, but it doesn't feel like me. I'd rather be talking about pleasant things or talking about something intelligible."

Western culture in particular has undervalued highly sensitive qualities in the workplace, arguably the environment where they are most needed. Ironically, an organization that places little or no value on these traits is undermining their own success. According to a 2011 study done by Bhavania Shrivastava, a work performance psychologist with the National Centre for High Sensitivity in the United Kingdom, people with higher sensory perception and processing ability are rated as the best performers by their managers.

You Are Valuable at Work

The combined qualities of intuition, creativity, empathy, and sensory perception and processing not only improve the organization's work environment, but also these qualities in an employee give the business an advantage over the competition when they are leveraged intelligently. Highly sensitive workers might be the first to falter in a toxic, aggressive work environment, but they will be the best employees in an environment that suits their temperaments.

Janine Ramsey, founder of the site Sensitivity Style (http://www.janineramsey.com.au/), says in an article for HRZone, "Organisations that create healthy environments and implement positive interventions for employees will see the greatest return on investment from their highly sensitive and perceptive employees."

Here are just some of the positive qualities sensitive people bring to their jobs. Highly sensitive employees . . .

- Are able to see the big picture, visionary.

- Tend to invest deeply in their work.

- Can think "outside the box."

- Can work well in a team environment.

- Care a lot about the outcome of their decisions.

- Pick up on emotions and tensions at the office before anyone else.

- Have the ability to make life easier for coworkers.

- Are conscientious, loyal, and dedicated.

- Can work independently with little supervision.

- Are detailed-oriented and organized.

- Have an inherent sense of fairness.

- Are excellent communicators.

- Avoid office politics.

- Avoid confrontation and conflict.

It's clear that in the right environment, HSPs (and empaths) can be extremely valuable employees and managers. If an organization appreciates what an HSP provides to the company, both the organization and the sensitive employee will thrive. An emotionally intelligent, open-minded manager would do well to accommodate the particular needs of his highly sensitive employee, as he or she will ultimately see results that far surpass any inconvenience or expense in doing so.

Managing Sensitives

If you are in a position of managing other people in your professional capacity, take the time to find out which of your employees are highly sensitive. Interview them individually and give them the HSP assessment by Dr. Aron (found at http://hsperson.com/test/highly-sensitive-test/). Ask them how you could structure their work environment, responsibilities, and interactions to support their innate traits, and discover what would make them feel motivated and inspired in their work. Be sure to reinforce that you find this trait a valuable asset to the organization, and do your best to play to the strengths of your sensitive employees.

Here are some changes you might consider:

- Allow the HSP employee to work in a private office or to work from home.

- Avoid micromanaging them or hovering over them as they work.

- Don't expect them to multitask well, or at least minimize your expectations about this.

- Allow them to work in softer, more natural light, rather than fluorescent lighting.

- Encourage them to take time for exercise, self-care, and vacations.

- Recognize that HSPs are people pleasers and might perform against their own natures in order to win approval.

- Pay attention to how your HSP employees are treated by other non-HSP employees, and don't allow a culture of incivility, verbal abuse, or bullying.

- Ask your HSPs to provide feedback on what's happening within the office or with your clients. HSPs are particularly tuned into nuances, and the well-being of your sensitive employees is a good indicator of the status of the overall working environment.

- If your HSP employee needs correction, have a calm and professional conversation with them, rather than raising your voice or using aggressive words.

- Don't assume your soft-spoken, non-confrontational HSP employee is weak, unmotivated, or disinterested. You'll find they perform at a high level with the right environment and management.

- An HSP might not be the "squeaky wheel" that you naturally reward, but don't overlook your HSP employees when it comes time for promotions or plum projects.

As the manager of HSPs, it's in your best interest and in the best interest of the organization to take care of your sensitive employees and provide them with the environment, resources, and support they need to be happy and productive on the job. Trying to force them to respond to an aggressive management style will cause undue stress for everyone, and you might eventually lose a highly valuable employee.

Managing Yourself as a Sensitive

If you are an HSP or empath employee, you must take the initiative to inform your manager and your coworkers about your traits. This can be intimidating if the culture of your office is anything but sensitive. But you must try, especially if the only alternatives are quitting or trying to survive in a toxic, overstimulating environment.

Show your boss the HSP assessment and your score on it. Remind him or her that high sensitivity is a normal personality trait and that you can do your best work when those traits are supported. Ask specifically for what you need—whether it's a calmer, quieter work environment or a reassignment to different work that better suits your nature. If you are being bullied or diminished by coworkers, tell your boss and ask that the behavior be addressed.

You might not get everything you ask for, but even incremental changes can make a big difference in how you feel at work and in your productivity. Over time, you can use your improved productivity to leverage more change and support from decision makers.

If you find yourself in a situation with your boss or a coworker in which they are talking aggressively or dismissively, you'll feel more confident and in control if you stand up for yourself and express how it makes you feel. "Joe, you don't need to speak so sharply to get me to work on the project. Just ask me calmly, and I'll be happy to help." "Sue, I'd like you to respect my input about these decisions. Please ask me the next time before you implement anything." Highly sensitive employees often get neglected or forgotten because they aren't loud and assertive in expressing their ideas or needs. Make sure you have a voice, even if it's a soft one.

If you are asked to do something that makes you extremely uncomfortable, you can speak up and say "no"—even if it means making someone else bristle. You don't have to compromise yourself in order to please everyone around you or to pretend you are assertive and bold. If this happens often, or you fear you might lose your job if you don't comply, then consider whether or not your job is the right fit for you.

As you become more aware of your sensitive and empathic traits and understand they are perfectly normal, you might come to the realization you are indeed in the wrong job or career field. This realization can be upsetting at first, but it can be wildly liberating when you recognize you aren't the "wrong person for the job," but rather you're in the wrong job for you.

"I have worked in the wrong profession for over 15 years," says my HSP reader, Charlotte. "I've been laid off or quit before being fired more times than I can count. After reading this [post], and looking back all the way to childhood, I see that my personality type combined with my careers have set me up for some bad choices." *You* don't have to keep making poor choices. You can find a career and work environment that's a great fit for you and one where your traits are highly valued.

Empath Challenges

Empaths have additional challenges to face in a traditional work environment. Because you're always tuned in to the feelings of those around you, you can feel bombarded and overwhelmed by the emotions coming at you from all directions. Over time coworkers might become aware of your empathic nature and turn into emotional vampires, using you to satisfy their neediness and frustrations.

As an empath, this behavior is particularly draining and difficult for you to deflect. Says my reader, Kate, "I work in a really awful environment with a lot of miserable people, and the angst gets to me so badly some days I can hardly move." Protecting yourself from the moods and negativity of those in your work environment can be a fulltime job. How do you focus on the tasks of your job when you feel saturated with distracting, unpleasant emotions?

One strategy is to arrive at work early before others do and perform your most pressing tasks first thing in the morning before you are impacted by the emotions of your coworkers. If it's allowed, wear headphones and play ambient, soothing music as you work so you don't overhear negative conversations.

If you have a private office, keep your door closed when you are working on projects that need complete focus. If you are in an open space or group setting, you might need to turn your back to avoid reading expressions or acknowledging the energy from others. However, you don't want to appear rude, so let your coworkers know you are going into a "work zone" for an hour or so in order to concentrate.

Because you are empathic, you might feel compelled to respond to the emotions of everyone around you. You might feel responsible for helping and supporting your coworkers when it's clear to you they need support. Give yourself permission to claim your job as a "hands off" environment when it comes to being the in-house therapist. Your job at work is to do the job you were hired to do. Offer your support outside of work if you feel inclined, or keep the name and number of a licensed counselor or coach handy that you can offer to your coworkers when they come to you for help. Protect yourself both for your mental health and for your ability to be productive at work.

If you're an empath in a leadership position and need to make objective, cool-headed decisions without allowing emotions to cloud your judgment, you might find your empathic nature makes it more difficult to be a strong leader. My empath reader, Paul, has experienced the conflict between his expected job duties and his empathic nature. "I am in a job where I come across a lot of people—I really do feel their pain, but I can't show them that I know and can't give comfort, as they see it as a public display of affection. In my line of work it is a complete dereliction of duty."

As a leader, you'll need to be particularly careful to rein in your desire to run in and save those around you. Try to maintain a professional distance between you and your employees, while still being kind, available, and supportive in an appropriate way. This is a difficult balance to strike for empaths, but it's not impossible if you set up a system for managing yourself and these situations as they arise.

Be prepared with a response when employees attempt to draw you into a conflict or emotional issue or when you start to sense their feelings. Suggest resources they might read or coaching that could be helpful. Set the tone in the office by directly communicating how conflict and personal problems should be handled. Set aside a specific time of day to meet with employees and address their concerns, but limit the amount of time you spend with them so you don't get overwhelmed or overly engaged.

Leaders can't dive into the emotional trenches with their employees and remain effective. The best way to lead and to manage your staff is by keeping your head clear so you can make sound decisions and take necessary actions in the best interest of your employer and everyone who works for and with you.

HSPs as Idealists

Whether you're a leader or worker bee, one of the most valuable HSP traits is the tendency to be idealists, to view the world not how it is, but how it could be. We want to feel like the work we do matters and makes a difference somehow. HSPs deeply desire to be appreciated, valued, and to feel a sense of purpose in their daily tasks.

Unfortunately, our idealistic philosophy isn't always compatible with corporate cultures that are more interested in the bottom line than in our efforts to improve things and save the world. However, in order to feel fulfilled in our careers, we *must* honor this idealistic trait by finding ways to express it in our work if at all possible.

If you haven't considered how your idealistic nature can be incorporated in your career, here are some questions to ponder:

- Are you happy with the work you do? (The daily activities of your job.)

- Does it feel like your passion, like you truly belong in this particular line of work?

- Do you feel like you're working toward something larger than just the profit of your employer?

- Do you feel respected, supported, and well-treated at work?

- Does your work environment make you want to be at work?

If you answered no to more than a couple of these questions, it might be time to reevaluate your situation and look for something that does light your fire. In the meantime, you can practice some coping strategies on the job right now to help you manage in a less-than-ideal situation:

- Create a morning routine that isn't stressful or rushed. Decide on your clothes the night before. Have everything ready to walk out the door. Arrive earlier so you aren't exhausted in the morning. Commit to a slower pace in the morning as a top a priority.

- Before you get out of bed, do some light stretching to get your blood flowing and help wake you up.

- Be sure to eat some protein in the morning, like a boiled egg, turkey bacon, or cottage cheese, and some toast with real butter, a bowl of granola with milk or a protein shake. For most HSPs, mornings can be overwhelming, so be sure to fuel up before you leave for work to keep your blood sugar balanced.

- Take healthy snacks with you to work (fruit, cheese, a granola bar) so you never feel too hungry at any point during the day.

- Even if you're a fashionista, find comfortable shoes to wear to work., especially if you're on your feet much of the day. Don't torture yourself with uncomfortable clothing (painful shoes, scratchy tags, suffocating sweaters), which feels excruciatingly irritating to an HSP.

- Try to avoid traffic by taking alternate routes or leaving home early. If you must sit in traffic, listen to soothing music or an uplifting CD.

- Make sure your chair at work is comfortable and ergonomically correct for the type of work you do. If you work at a computer, your eyes should be focused at about two inches below the top of your screen, which prevents you from craning your neck up or down while reading.

- When you're at work and start to feel stressed or overwhelmed during the day, take a break and move to a different environment. Take a short walk outside or go to the restroom and take a few deep breaths.

- Work off negative energy and anxiety by doing something physical. If you can't go for a walk, just stand up and stretch, walk in place, roll your shoulders and neck. You can even get on the floor and do a few pushups. Moving your body releases some of that negative energy and gives you a sense of control.

- Define and create your boundaries at work. Don't allow people to interrupt you or play loud music nearby. Learn to say "no" when you don't have time to do something for someone else. Don't accept being spoken to rudely or being bypassed or neglected. Learn to speak up for yourself, even if it's uncomfortable.

- Reduce stress and work pressure by planning extra time "padding" to complete a project. Be sure to communicate with your boss or clients to manage their expectations about the amount of time a project will take you.

- Break down large projects into manageable chunks that don't feel so overwhelming. Take small breaks to recharge after you finish one chunk before you begin another.

- Remind yourself not to feel guilty or shamed about your work style as an HSP. You are working *more* productively by honoring who you are, even if those around you don't seem to get it.

If you think you might be in the wrong job or career field, make it a priority to research and investigate a job that's a better fit for you. You might not know exactly what kind of work you feel passionate about, so read this article ("25 Action Steps for Transitioning to Your Life Passion"— http://liveboldandbloom.com/03/career/25-action-steps-for-transitioning-to-your-life-passion) on my blog to learn some of the steps to help you figure it out. I've also written a book (*The 52-Week Life Passion Project)* and a course ("The Path to Passion, Love What You Do"a— http://pathtopassioncourse.com/) helping people find their life passions. Until you find work you feel passionate about, make *the process* of finding your passion your life passion for now.

The Right Career for You

Look for careers that allow some downtime throughout the day so you can recuperate from long projects and stimulating environments or encounters. Be sure the work fits well with your idealistic nature and your desire to do something meaningful and fulfilling. Empaths should be particularly aware of the personalities of the people they will be working for and around. The manager generally sets the tone for the behavior and demeanor of employees, so pay close attention to his or her management style. Use your empathic skills to discern if you feel drained or enlivened around your prospective boss and coworkers.

When you are interviewing for a job, don't hesitate to ask questions of your future employer to determine whether or not the environment, culture, and management style is right for you. This might be uncomfortable, but you'll save yourself a lot of heartache by finding out this information before you accept a job.

Job interviews are nerve-racking for all of us, and HSPs are even more susceptible to anxiety and pre-interview jitters. An interview can be one of the most stressful and overstimulating events for HSPs, but with some preparation and forethought, you can get through it confidently.

Know what you want to ask in advance, and thoroughly prepare your answers to anticipated questions. Then rehearse your answers out loud in front of a mirror. During the actual interview, *pretend* that you're confident, poised and articulate, acting "as if" you are self-assured, even if you're really nervous. Throughout the interview, take several deep breaths and smile often, which will make you feel calmer.

Working for Yourself

I've worked in several corporate environments, and ¡
been more suited to my HSP traits than others. However, I've
found the best career for me is one in which I'm my own boss.
Many HSPs and empaths ultimately choose to work for
themselves or become consultants so they can manage their own
schedules and work environments.

My current career as an author, blogger, coach, and online
teacher has proven to be perfect for me as an HSP. I work from
home on my own schedule, in a peaceful and calm environment. I
can take breaks to exercise or meditate whenever I want, and I
don't have anyone breathing down my neck or watching the clock.

The nature of my work is creative and meaningful. I know I'm
helping others and leaving a positive legacy. However, none of
this happened by accident. I worked for several years trying to
figure out exactly what I felt passionate about and then how to
build a homed-based business around it. (See
http://workfromhomeduo.com/.) Everyone deserves the time to
figure this out, especially highly sensitive people. So give yourself
the gift of this time so you can work in alignment with your innate
traits and find the fulfillment you so crave in your career.

If you feel confident in your ability and willingness to speak up for
what you need in your current job and have an accommodating
boss, then you can thrive in just about any career as an HSP or
empath. However, you might want to consider a career in which
you control as many of the variables as possible. This means
either working for a flexible organization or working for yourself.

Even though HSPs prefer a calm, less-stimulating environment,
that doesn't mean we'll settle for boring. We want to have variety

n our work and to feel challenged in positive ways. We want to utilize our creativity, organizational skills, and desire to make a difference.

Here are some good careers to consider for empaths and HSPs:

Accountant

Actor

Analyst

Animal care

Architect

Artist

Business owner

Clergy

Coach

Consultant

Counselor

Customer service

Detective

Editor

Education

Engineer

Entrepreneur

Finely Tuned

✓ Fashion designer

✓ Florist

   Graphic designer

✓ Healing professions

   Interior designer

   Investigator

   Librarian

✓ Massage therapist

   Music teacher

   Musician

   Perfume tester

   Personal assistant

   Photographer

   Programmer

✓ Researcher

   Sales

   Social worker

   Tutor

   Virtual Assistant

✓ Writer

If you do decide to become self-employed, remember it will be easy to isolate yourself. You'll need to be proactive about reaching out to friends and socializing. This is particularly true for empaths who feel so easily overwhelmed by the feelings and moods of other people. Loneliness can be as crippling as emotional deluge, so make a point to find friends and business associates who respect your gifts and possess strong emotional intelligence. See "5 Ways to Boost Emotional Intelligence in the Workplace" (link to website located in Reference section).

Even though you might feel uncomfortable marketing yourself or your goods or services, you'll have to stretch yourself to do so, if you want to make a living. Consider joining networking groups, both online and in real life, and connect with others who are successfully self-employed.

You might not be in the position right now to become self-employed or change jobs in order to do what you love. You might discover you can't make enough money at your passion to justify leaving a secure position in the short term. If this is the case for you, then you'll have to continue working at a less-than-desirable job in order to take care of your financial and family obligations. But while you are waiting, be sure to put money aside and save for making a change down the road.

You can start right now taking other small steps toward your ideal job. Update your résumé, refresh your skills, or go back to school if necessary. Research interesting jobs, and interview people who are successfully doing what you'd like to do. As you consider the kind of job that might be best for you as an HSP, ask yourself these questions:

1. On a 1–10 scale, with 10 being totally fulfilling and enjoyable and 1 being completely dissatisfying, how would you rate your current job?

2. What elements of your current job do you enjoy and value that you would want to maintain in any future career? List everything you can think of, including your commute time, the physical environment, the people you work with, etc.

3. What elements of your current job would you wish to completely avoid in any future job?

4. Do you know or have an inkling about the kind of work that would excite and fulfill you and that would support your HSP traits?

5. If so, why have you not pursued this work or found a career in it?

6. If not, would you be willing and able to invest a few hours a week for research and self-discovery to find the type of work that would excite you?

7. Do you currently live within your financial means and have a cushion of savings?

8. If not, would you be willing to adjust your lifestyle and spending habits to live within your means and/or save money?

9. If so, what elements of your current lifestyle are more important to you than job satisfaction? List everything that trumps job satisfaction for you (that is, children's education, taking care of elderly parents, living in a particular neighborhood or house).

10. Would you be willing to downsize your home for a job you love?

11. Would you be willing to move to another city for a job you love?

12. Would you be willing to disappoint or upset someone close to you to change careers for a job you love?

13. Is there anything you could change about your current job that would make it more fulfilling and workable for your HSP traits?

14. What are the possible consequences of asking for change at your current job? Could you live with those consequences?

15. If you were to lose your current job today, what would you do?

16. How long could you maintain your current lifestyle if you were unemployed?

17. If you were starting over right out of school, what career would you pursue?

18. Would you be willing and/or able to get additional education or training for a job you love?

19. Would your spouse support you in a career change?

20. Would your spouse be willing to make lifestyle sacrifices in order for you to make a career change?

21. What have you done toward finding a job or career that you love? (that is, research, updating your résumé, looking at job openings, etc.)

22. How could you find or create the time to research and/or look for a job you love?

23. In the past, when have you felt the most fulfilled and happy in your personal and professional life?

24. If you were writing a vision for your ideal life and work, what would it look like?

25. Do you believe it is possible to create your life in a way that is close to that ideal?

26. If you were aged 90, looking back on your life, what would you like to have accomplished personally and professionally?

27. Would you be willing and able to try out a few jobs before you found one that is deeply fulfilling?

28. Do you feel like you know yourself well enough to know what makes you happy and fulfilled? If not, where do you need some self-discovery work?

29. Do you have beliefs or fears about yourself or your abilities that prevent you from acting? If so, how could you begin to address these?

30. What is the least amount of money you'd be willing to make?

31. What is most important to you, job satisfaction or prestige?

32. How is your dissatisfaction with your current job impacting the rest of your life? (that is, stress, relationships, life balance, etc.)

33. If you didn't have to work at all, what would you do?

34. What one thing could you do today to move toward finding work you love that supports your highly sensitive nature?

Here are some ways you can use these questions and your answers to begin making a shift toward finding work you love.

- Look at all of the "non-negotiables" you have listed in your answers. Are they absolutely non-negotiable or is there any wiggle room? Think about how these will impact your potential career change.

- Review the areas you listed that you enjoy and find fulfilling in life and work. Where do you see a pattern? How can these areas translate into a career?

- Think realistically about the potential lifestyle changes that would be involved in finding and taking a job that would make you really happy and feel supported as an HSP. For example, would you be willing to sell your house, pack up and move, and live more frugally if it meant you could be happy most of the day, every day?

- If you are unsure about the kind of work you would feel passionate about, take the time to do some self-discovery work. Read books, take courses, take some career assessments, and meet with a career coach or counselor.

- Talk with your significant other, friends, or family members to discuss your ideas and the potential repercussions and necessary actions involved in changing careers.

Even when highly sensitive people find their passions, they are often underemployed in relation to their education, intelligence, and experience. This occurs either because their less-assertive, unassuming natures prevent them from being noticed at work, or because their creative leanings lead them to traditionally lower-paying professions, such as the arts. By getting clear on the answers to the questions listed previously, you can determine what your priorities are, where you need to focus your efforts, and how far you're willing to stretch yourself to get what you want.

For me, I prioritize doing work I love in an environment that supports my HSP traits, even if it means making less money than I might make in a corporate job. Leaving the security of regular fulltime employment was scary, but for me, it was far less scary than working in a job that caused anxiety and unhappiness. You might even discover that once you are doing passionate work in the right environment, you *can* have it all—a great job, a great income, career fulfillment, and happiness.

If you have some personal challenges holding you back from taking charge of your career, related to self-esteem, self-doubt, or your HSP traits, make an appointment with a counselor to address these proactively. Don't allow yourself to remain stuck in a job that is slowly killing you or making you miserable. Now you know how to thrive in your career as an HSP and what to do to find a job suitable to your amazing qualities, so you don't need to accept anything less. You spend far too much time at work not to make this career goal a top priority in your life.

Chapter 11: Managing Daily Life as an HSP and Empath

When I first learned about highly sensitive people and empaths and understood more about the traits, I was blown away. It was profoundly enlightening and validating to realize my sensitivity wasn't a weakness. I thought about all the times I'd felt embarrassed because of my sensitive nature. I thought about the people who had unknowingly or overtly criticized me for being too sensitive.

I thought about all the coping strategies I'd crafted in order to perform well at work, fit in with the crowd, or appear in control and confident. I thought about the emotional and mental energy I put into these efforts, energy I could have spent on more fulfilling, positive pursuits. However, an amazing thing happened once I recognized myself as an HSP and realized being sensitive was not only normal but a gifted trait. Over time, I naturally felt more confident, self-assured, and happy with myself. I no longer had to apologize for my nature or work to accommodate my lifestyle choices to match what I thought I *should* be. It was such a relief.

Being an HSP is no more unusual than being left-handed or having red hair. But HSPs are still in the minority, and that means we need to create life strategies to maximize our gifts and our enjoyment of them—and to minimize overstimulation and discomfort. We don't need to apologize for managing our lives this way, no more than a left-handed person should apologize for needing left-handed scissors. We all have differences that make us unique and require us to adapt in special ways.

Now that you see yourself as an HSP or an empath and recognize the ways you've unknowingly undermined or disparaged your sensitive traits, you might feel overwhelmed with the knowledge. Maybe you recognize the negative habits you've developed over the years to hide your true nature and to cope with your sensitivities. It's natural to feel overwhelmed with this awareness, even though it's good news. You can't expect yourself to change overnight. It will take time to fully embrace who you are and to change your mind set and behaviors.

The biggest question that comes up at this point is, "Where do I begin?" How do you start living life "out of the closet" as a sensitive person without rocking your entire world? As with any big life change, you begin with one small step at a time. Every sensitive person is different in the ways he or she has managed or hidden their traits.

Some might find they feel accepted and supported with friends and family, but they must behave differently at work. Others might have family dynamics where they were shamed because of their sensitivities but otherwise they can be themselves. Maybe you are someone who already embraces your unique traits, but you need strategies to help with overstimulation and hypersensitivity in specific situations.

In each chapter of this book, I've offered ideas for managing your life to support your gift of sensitivity in different areas of life. However, you might find it helpful to review a full list of strategies and suggestions so you can readily see the best actions to support you on your journey as a highly sensitive person and/or empath.

Read through the suggestions listed here, and pick one or two to begin working on right away. Some actions will be easy to implement, but others you might find more challenging. Do what feels manageable for you now, but try to stretch yourself slightly beyond your comfort zone. Continue adding changes to your daily routines, choices, and interactions as you become more confident in who you are and what you need to feel happy and fulfilled in life.

Mind Set Changes

- Remind yourself daily that being a highly sensitive person is a normal trait. You are as normal as your less-sensitive friends and family. Remember all the scientific research, from Dr. Aron and others, that proves this.

- Review all the positive qualities of HSPs listed in Chapter 3 of this book. Begin to see your sensitive traits as a gift rather than a weakness. Create an affirmation, like "My sensitivities empower my creativity, intuition, and awareness, and my life is richer as a result." Write and speak your affirmation several times a day to reinforce your new outlook.

- Work on accepting that you are not "lesser than" your more-assertive, less-sensitive friends, family, or work associates. Others might not appreciate the value of your sensitivities, but there is not one right or wrong way to be.

- Because HSPs are in the minority, we are charged with educating others about our sensitivities and needs. Remind yourself that you can't expect others to automatically understand or support you unless you communicate with them.

- Believe that you can gently push yourself beyond your level of discomfort about your sensitivities. You can ask for what you want, express how you feel, and be your authentic self. With practice, you will feel more and more confident and self-accepting.

- Whether you're a man or woman, crying is OK. When emotions bubble up, and you need to cry, allow it to happen. Suppressing these feelings can lead to other physical and emotional difficulties.

Daily Routine

- Wake up early enough to allow yourself plenty of time to get dressed, eat a healthy breakfast, and prepare for your day at a leisurely pace.

- If you set an alarm to awaken you, make sure it is a gentle, soothing sound rather than a blaring buzzer or bell. Allow a few extra minutes in bed to awaken, stretch, and get up slowly.

- Plan what you are going to wear the night before and have it clean, pressed, and ready to put on in the morning.

- Perform some light exercise in the morning, such as yoga or stretching to get you moving.

- Spend five to ten minutes in meditation, contemplation, prayer, or read something inspirational and uplifting.

Finely Tuned

- Eat a healthy, nourishing breakfast and be mindful of your coffee consumption. Switch to herbal tea if caffeine causes agitation.

- If you take medications in the morning, be sure to take them with food to avoid or minimize unpleasant reactions or stomach problems.

- If you are married or have a partner, ask them to give you a long affectionate hug before you leave for the day.

- Take a route to work that has the least amount of traffic and noise, even if it takes you slightly longer.

- On the way to work, listen to calm, soothing music or an uplifting podcast or audio. Avoid the news or loud abrasive music.

- In the evening, plan activities that are calming, such as reading uplifting books, writing, walking, preparing a meal, meditating, taking a bath, or having light discussions.

- Avoid watching disturbing or overstimulating TV programs in the evening, especially right before bed.

- Go to bed early enough to allow for a full eight to nine hours of sleep at night so you feel completely rested in the morning.

- Have a regular bedtime routine that feels comforting, such as taking a bath, drinking a cup of herbal tea, and reading a book just before falling asleep.

Protecting Your Senses

- Wear earplugs and eye shades if necessary when you sleep to block out noise and light that might keep you awake.

- Invest in a sound machine or "white noise" app on your iPhone to drown out extraneous noise at work or when trying to fall asleep.

- Find music that is soothing or uplifting to use as a background while you work or at home when preparing meals, reading, or working on a project.

- If others around you are disturbing you with their noise, politely ask them to keep it down or move to another room. Try moving to a quieter space yourself if necessary.

- Design one room in your house as a peaceful sanctuary where you can spend quiet time when you need to withdraw periodically to get a break from an overload of external stimulation. Make sure the room is free of clutter and has a comfortable space to sit with soft lighting.

- Several times a day, close your eyes and focus on your breathing for a few minutes.

- Keep your home and work spaces clear of clutter and mess. Create visual harmony and simplicity where you work and live. See "How to Simplify Your Life: 50 Actions to Foster Peace and Contentment" (link to website located in Reference section).

- Arrange your desk or workspace near a window so you can look outside frequently. If that's not possible, take breaks during the day so you can look outside or go for a brief walk.

- Have plants and flowers in your home and office.

- Regularly spend time in beauty and nature by taking hikes, walks, runs, and bike rides.

- Choose calming colors for your home and office, such as greens, blues, and neutrals. Flip through a home magazine and pay attention to the rooms that make you feel calm and happy and those that tend to agitate you.

- Try to use incandescent lighting or other warm or natural light sources rather than fluorescent lighting at home and work. Test various types of lighting to see what feels best for you.

- Invest in blackout curtains for your bedroom to block light when you are sleeping.

- Keep several pair of sunglasses available at home, in your car, and at work.

- Use an air purifier in your home and at work to reduce bad odors. Request an office space away from food smells, smoking areas, or coworkers who wear heavy perfume or cologne.

- If someone close to you wears an offensive scent, kindly ask them if they'd be willing to stop wearing it around you. Explain why you are sensitive to smells.

- If you have pets, bathe them frequently and keep their food in an area where you can't smell it. Change cat litter boxes frequently.

- Use soothing oils or incense, such as sandalwood, lavender, jasmine, or rose.

- Get regular massages and/or facials from a professional or someone you love. Ask for regular affectionate touch and hugs from your spouse or partner.

- Wear clothing that is soft and comfortable. Cut out scratchy tags and labels. Layer clothing so you can manage your body temperature.

- Wear shoes that are comfortable. Avoid wearing heels or other shoes that cause your feet pain throughout the day, even if they look great. Or keep comfortable shoes at your desk and put them on when you're not in public.

- Be sure you have a comfortable chair for work and that your chair is ergonomically suitable to your desk and computer height. You can read more about choosing the best desk chair at "The Definitive Guide to Choosing an Office Chair" by Patrick Jobin.

- Take warm baths or showers using essential oils.

- Maintain steady blood sugar levels throughout the day with regular, healthy, well-balanced meals and snacks. Eat foods known to calm anxiety, such as whole grains, berries, almonds, fish with omega-3 fatty acids (wild salmon, herring, trout, and sardines), dark chocolate, apples, oranges, and bananas.

- Minimize your consumption of caffeine and alcohol.

- Notice how the temperatures of different foods affect you and adjust accordingly.

- Pay attention to emotional eating as a way of self-soothing. If you notice you do this, try to switch to a healthier way to calm yourself through meditation or exercise.

Body Sensations and Pain

- Notice when you feel tired or physically drained and don't force yourself to push through it. Honor your body and the messages it is sending you, and allow yourself to rest.

- Pay attention to other physical signals your body is sending through illness, pain, or discomfort. Notice whether there's an emotional trigger connected to your physical feelings and address the emotional trigger.

- Notice how you feel after taking medications and discern if you think you are taking the correct medication or dosage. Talk with your doctor about any usual or unpleasant symptoms and ask for an adjustment if necessary.

- Pay attention to how chemicals, dyes, and cleaning agents make you feel physically. Try to find natural alternatives for these products or do without them if possible.

- Let your physician or dentist know about your pain sensitivity before any procedures and ask that you receive pain relief if you request it. Don't suffer with pain because you feel embarrassed.

- Simply going to the doctor is enough to cause stress and overwhelm for an HSP. Share information about HSPs with your doctor and let him or her know how appointments make you feel. Ask for what you need from your doctor in order to feel less stressed. Or find a doctor who has a more caring, personal approach.

- If you suffer normal aches and pains (from exercise, menstruation, headache, colds, and flu) more intensely than most people, find alternative ways of dealing with your pain aside from increasing medications. Read this article from Dr. Aron about coping with pain. See "Ways to Deal with Serious Pain beyond Medication" (link to website located in Reference section).

- Pay attention to how your body feels after extended use of the computer, cell phone, or other electronic equipment. Notice whether or not it stresses or depletes your energy, and dial back your time on these devices if so.

- If you have asthma or allergic responses, pay attention to possible emotional or environmental triggers and try to manage these if you can.

- Stress from constant overwhelm and overstimulation can appear in a wide variety of symptoms, from chronic fatigue to irritable bowel. If you have unexplained physical symptoms, closely examine how your sensitivities might be chronically disrupted or agitated. Try to change the source of the agitation to see if you can heal the symptoms.

Emotional and Mental Health

- Recognize that HSPs are more prone to anxiety and depression than the average population. Be sure you know the signs of depression, and that you seek treatment with your physician and talk therapist right away. See "Just a Bad Mood or Are You Coming Unglued?" (link to website located in Reference section).

- If you had a difficult or traumatic childhood, or if your parents criticized your sensitivities, find a talk therapist who is familiar with the sensitivity trait to work on healing your emotional pain from these past events.

- Reduce stress and overwhelm by simplifying all aspects of your life. Cut back on obligations, commitments, tasks, and projects. Pare down to the most essential and enjoyable activities. Stop answering every text, email, or phone call right away.

- Pay attention to how much you rely on the opinion of others for your own self-esteem. Notice times you people please or change your behavior in order to feel good about yourself.

- Try to accept that it's OK to limit your exposure to people and situations in order to protect your mental and emotional health. Think about who or what triggers feelings of overstimulation and stress and develop a plan for disengaging.

- Find a way to channel your sensitivities and feelings through a creative outlet, such as art, music, writing, etc. Allow yourself to express the depth of your feelings in your craft.

- Because HSPs react so strongly to criticism, even kind and constructive criticism, we tend to have a defensive, emotional response to it. Practice waiting a day before you respond to criticism. Use your judgment (rather than emotions) to discern if the criticism has merit and if you can learn from it.

- When you feel down or anxious, proactively focus on things that make you feel positive and happy. Put yourself in positive, uplifting situations with people who are caring and supportive.

- Don't allow your sensitive traits to serve as a crutch or excuse for not addressing emotional or mental health issues or for working on improving your ability to cope. Having a trait doesn't mean all your reactions and behaviors are set in stone.

- Begin a regular mindfulness practice (like meditation) in order to manage stress and overstimulation. I've outlined the steps for a regular mindfulness meditation. See "Mindfulness Meditation: The Path to Inner Peace and Health" (link to website located in Reference section).

- Get a weekly massage. Massage has been shown to reduce cortisol levels (stress hormones) and decrease the arousal level of the sympathetic nervous system.

Managing Relationships

- Proactively communicate with the most important people in your life about what it means to be a highly sensitive person. Be specific in asking them how they can support you.

- Remember, you will also need to compromise your expectations and behaviors in your relationships. Open and regular communication is the best way to navigate compromise and prevent hurt feelings or anger.

- Give your loved ones the benefit of the doubt when they say or do something that offends or wounds you. Practice waiting before reacting, and then clarify the other person's intentions.

- Find other highly sensitive friends who have found ways to leverage their unique gifts to add to their life happiness, success, and fulfillment. Learn from them and try to emulate their strategies for thriving.

- Practice gratitude in your relationships by choosing to focus on what you appreciate about your partner and the other close people in your life.

- Define your relationship boundaries and communicate them with others. Pay attention to your tendency to "people please" or to give too much, and take care of yourself by stepping back.

- Don't ignore the "red flags" that your sensitivity and intuition signal to you about a relationship. If you don't feel comfortable or safe around someone, let them go quickly. Find support to help you do this if necessary.

- Learn conflict resolution skills so you are prepared to calmly address problems that occur in your relationships rather than reacting to your emotions. See "Conflict Resolution Skills" (link to website located in Reference section).

- Allow yourself "personal space time" in your love relationship to be alone and recharge when you feel overwhelmed or agitated. Be sure you communicate your need for this with your partner and remind him or her it doesn't mean you want to pull away.

- Be proactive, rather than reactive, in your choices of romantic partners and close friends. Define what you want and value in these relationships and seek out the people you want in life, rather than passively accepting anyone who comes your way.

- If you are in a toxic relationship or live with toxic people whose presence makes you feel anxious, physically ill, or fearful, you must leave. You are feeling the negative effects of their toxicity far more than the average person.

- Continue to research and learn about the qualities of emotionally intelligent, self-aware, and mentally healthy people so that you know what you are looking for in a friend or partner. See "Embrace Your Inner Adult" (link to website located in Reference section).

- Work on your own self-awareness and personal growth by reading, researching, and talking with a coach or therapist. See "Self-Awareness: 30 Essential Actions for Living Authentically" (link to website located in Reference section).

Thriving at Work

- Even if you can't change jobs or careers immediately, work on finding your passion and look for ways to enjoy and practice your passion outside of work through a hobby or side gig.

- Do whatever you can to manage your physical work environment to minimize overwhelm and excess stimulation. Talk to your boss about what you need and ask for it. Even a few changes can make a big difference in how you feel.

- Practice speaking up more at work by proactively sharing ideas, making suggestions, and letting decision makers know about your successes and abilities. This might be uncomfortable, but you will feel empowered when you are heard and acknowledged.

- Find ways to use your gifts on the job to increase your enjoyment at work, and also to improve or benefit your organization. Share ideas with your boss about how your gifts could be better utilized to benefit the company.

- If you are miserable at work, do everything in your power to extricate yourself as quickly as possible. Begin to save money, update your résumé, hone your skills, go back to school—whatever it takes to break free. Don't settle for a job you hate.

- Protect yourself from the emotions, conflicts, and neediness of people around you at work. Stay focused on your work, and carefully choose your confidants and friends at work. Create positive, enjoyable social interactions at work that don't drain you.

Other Tips

- Define your own core values and use those as a guideline for making choices and decisions. Prioritize your own values, rather than looking outside yourself for validation or direction. Use this list of 400 value words to help you. See "400 Value Words" (link to Website located in Reference section).

- Smile often. Find enjoyment in simple activities, such as preparing a meal, taking a walk, and spending time with friends and family. Learn what makes you relaxed and happy and do more of those things.

- Pay attention to feelings of boredom and proactively do something innovative, creative, or different to shake yourself out of apathy or inertia.

- Keep a dream journal next to your bed and write down your dreams as soon as you remember them. Sensitive people tend to have vivid dreams, which can be enlightening and helpful in processing feelings.

- Because of our depth of processing, HSPs often have a difficult time making decisions and agonize over choices. When you make decisions, do your research, weigh the pros and cons, and seek trusted advice. Give yourself plenty of time to make the decision and visualize all possible outcomes to feel where you are most comfortable.

- Explore a wide variety of creative pursuits, even if you've never tried them before. Allow yourself to experiment even if you aren't "perfect" or accomplished. You might be surprised at the pleasure you discover.

- Maintain routines. In a chaotic, unpredictable world, routines provide security and comfort. Try to stick to your daily routines, particularly when you have disruptions or discord in your life.

- When you travel, think through possible difficulties and ways you might experience sensory overload. Prepare in advance for those if you can. For example, bring headphones and eye shades to the airport. Arrive early to avoid traffic and stress. Ask for a quiet room in hotels. Visit attractions during the least crowded times.

- Get a pet or spend time with animals as much as possible. Sensitive people tend to have a deep and rewarding connection with animals.

- Watch your language for chronic self-criticism or self-deprecation, people-pleasing comments, and inauthenticity. Learn to speak your truth kindly and confidently.

- Try to be a role model and emissary for sensitive people and/or empaths. Educate nonsensitives and sensitives alike about the traits and gifts of HSPs and empaths. Let others know that the traits are normal and positive. Show people through your actions and words that sensitivity isn't a weakness but rather a gift that you highly value.

All change begins with awareness, and if you've reached this point in the book, you are now aware of some important truths about your sensitive nature. You are normal. You are gifted. You can thrive as an empath or HSP.

But awareness alone doesn't create change. You must combine this awareness with action that feels comfortable for you. Where do *you* struggle most as a sensitive person? Start there and every single day implement some of the strategies outlined in this book. Your new awareness affords a huge opportunity to grow as a person, build your self-confidence, improve your relationships, and maximize your joy in life. Don't just read this book and ponder what you've learned. Do something!

If you really don't know what to do first, begin by sharing the facts about HSPs and empaths with the people closest to you. Just the smallest change in the attitude of those around you can help you feel understood and validated. Sometimes you need to show people the research in order for them to accept the truth of what you are telling them. They need to hear it from a "professional," so have the research and facts available to share. It might take time for your loved ones to fully understand your traits, so be patient and continue to gently remind them.

Now when people say to me, "Don't be so sensitive," I've learned to respond by saying, "But I am sensitive, and proudly so. You'll have to accept me as I am." I no longer make excuses for my feelings and reactions, nor do I try to deflect blame to the other person for being insensitive. We are simply two people who view situations differently, and if we are both motivated, we can find common ground and compromise. That's essential for all healthy relationships.

If you have suffered a great deal in your life as a result of your sensitivities and the way you have been treated because of them, try to be particularly kind and patient with yourself. It is extremely helpful to reframe your past experiences in light of your new understanding about your innate sensitive nature. Many of the difficulties, conflicts, and failures you experienced were unavoidable because neither you nor your parents, teachers, friends, and colleagues really understood you. Reframing the past and accepting you weren't at fault or faulty in some way helps bolster your self-esteem, which is so important for sensitive people to possess.

You might find it difficult to address the wounds from the past and seek psychotherapy or support of some kind, because you know the intense feelings that will arise as a result. However, it's extremely important you do the inner work necessary for healing so you can savor the gifts of being a sensitive person. Don't cheat yourself of the fulfilling and happy life you deserve.

As a sensitive person—an HSP, empath, or both—you were born with traits that might have caused you intense pain and sorrow, but which also provide richly satisfying, creative, and joy-filled experiences. As the poet Kahlil Gibran reminds in his book *The Prophet*, "Your joy is your sorrow unmasked. And the selfsame well from which your laughter rises was oftentimes filled with your tears." Joy and sorrow are part of the human condition, but highly sensitive people are in the unique position to experience both more intensely.

Perhaps this poem, "The Invitation," by Oriah Mountain Dreamer, best expresses the exquisite juxtaposition of joy and pain in our sensitive natures.

The Invitation by Oriah

It doesn't interest me
what you do for a living.
I want to know
what you ache for
and if you dare to dream
of meeting your heart's longing.

It doesn't interest me
how old you are.
I want to know
if you will risk
looking like a fool
for love
for your dream
for the adventure of being alive.

Barrie Davenport

It doesn't interest me
what planets are
squaring your moon...
I want to know
if you have touched
the centre of your own sorrow
if you have been opened
by life's betrayals
or have become shrivelled and closed
from fear of further pain.

I want to know
if you can sit with pain
mine or your own
without moving to hide it
or fade it
or fix it.

I want to know
if you can be with joy
mine or your own
if you can dance with wildness
and let the ecstasy fill you
to the tips of your fingers and toes
without cautioning us
to be careful
to be realistic
to remember the limitations
of being human.

It doesn't interest me
if the story you are telling me
is true.
I want to know if you can
disappoint another
to be true to yourself.
If you can bear
the accusation of betrayal

Finely Tuned

and not betray your own soul.
If you can be faithless
and therefore trustworthy.

I want to know if you can see Beauty
even when it is not pretty
every day.
And if you can source your own life
from its presence.

I want to know
if you can live with failure
yours and mine
and still stand at the edge of the lake
and shout to the silver of the full moon,
"Yes."

It doesn't interest me
to know where you live
or how much money you have.
I want to know if you can get up
after the night of grief and despair
weary and bruised to the bone
and do what needs to be done
to feed the children.

It doesn't interest me
who you know
or how you came to be here.
I want to know if you will stand
in the centre of the fire
with me
and not shrink back.

It doesn't interest me
where or what or with whom
you have studied.
I want to know

Barrie Davenport

what sustains you
from the inside
when all else falls away.

I want to know
if you can be alone
with yourself
and if you truly like
the company you keep
in the empty moments.

The purpose of this book has been to help you *thrive* as a
sensitive person, someone whose sensibilities and intuition are
more finely tuned than the average person. By managing and
altering your choices, reactions, and environments, you can
minimize your overwhelm, pain, and grief. But I believe as
sensitives, we are called to experience the inevitable suffering that
comes with being finely tuned as an invitation to deeper self-
awareness, compassion, and love.

Rather than resisting pain when it arrives, we can learn to
embrace it as a pathway to full living. To be genuinely,
unabashedly alive, we must allow ourselves to be vulnerable, and
being vulnerable opens us to the possibility of pain. As we learn to
accept the co-presence of joy and suffering, we become fully open
to the inexhaustible beauty of the world.

Our heightened experience of this beauty is a rare gift indeed,
reserved for those of us who feel more deeply, love more

intensely, and savor the subtle, trembling nuances of life all around us.

References

"Conflict Resolution Skills: Building the Skills That Can Turn Conflicts into Opportunities." See http://www.helpguide.org/articles/relationships/conflict-resolution-skills.htm

"Genes Affect Anxiety and Startle Response," American Psychological Association press release, August 18, 2008. See http://talentdevelop.com/articlelive/articles/761/1/Genes-affect-anxiety-and-startle-response/Page1.html

Acevedo, Bianca P., Elaine N. Aron, Arthur Aron, Matthew-Donald Sangster, Nancy Collins, and Lucy L. Brown, "The Highly Sensitive Brain: An fMRI Study of Sensory Processing Sensitivity and Response to Others' Emotions," *Brain and Behavior,* Open Access, 2014. See http://hsperson.com/pdf/The_highly_sensitive_brain_%20an_fMRI_study.pdf

Aron, Elaine, "The Clinical Implications of Jung's Concept of Sensitiveness," Journal of Jungian Theory and Practice, 8, (2006), 16. See http://www.junginstitute.org/pdf_files/JungV8N2p11-44.pdf

Aron, Elaine, "A Few 'Happy' Things Regarding Depression," February 2010. See http://www.hsperson.com/pages/2Feb10.htm#pdf

Aron, Elaine, "For Highly Sensitive Teenagers, Part IV: Friendships," November 2008. See http://www.hsperson.com/pages/2Nov08.htm

Aron, Elaine, *The Highly Sensitive Person* (New York: Carol Publishing Company, 1996).

Aron, Elaine, "The Highly Sensitive Person in Love," See http://hsperson.com/books/the-highly-sensitive-person-in-love/

Aron, Elaine, "On Having an Invisible yet Definitive Part of Yourself," The Comfort Zone website (December 3, 2014). See http://hsperson.com/invisible-yet-definitive-part-of-yourself/

Aron, Elaine, "Ways to Deal with Serious Pain beyond Medication." See http://www.hsperson.com/pages/1Feb12.htm

Aron, Elaine, quote in "Sensitive? Emotional? Empathetic? It Could be in Your Genes," Stony Brook University Medical Center and Health Care Newsroom (June 23, 2014). See http://sb.cc.stonybrook.edu/news/medical/140623empathet icAron.php#sthash.eF31nkos.dpuf regarding: Acevedo, Bianca P., Elaine N. Aron, Arthur Aron, Matthew-Donald Sangster, Nancy Collins, and Lucy L. Brown, "The Highly Sensitive Brain: An fMRI Study of Sensory Processing Sensitivity and Response to Others' Emotions," *Brain and Behavior,* Open Access, 2014.

Aron, Elaine, and Arthur Aron, "HSP Scale," 1996. See http://hsperson.com/test/highly-sensitive-test/

Belden, Rick, "I Am a Highly Sensitive Man," The Good Men Project, November 26, 2012. See http://goodmenproject.com/featured-content/the-good-life-i-am-a-highly-sensitive-man/

Belden, Rick, Iron Man Family Outing: Poems about Transition into a More Conscious Manhood (Richard M. Belden, 1990).

Belsky, Jay, "Differential Susceptibility to Environmental Influences," Birkbeck, University of London (November 17, 2010). See http://www.med.uio.no/klinmed/forskning/sentre/seraf/aktu elt/arrangementer/konferanser/konferanser-2010/presentasjoner-children-at-risk/Jay%20Belsky_Differential%20Susceptibility%20to%2 0environmental%20influences.pdf

Blakemore, Sarah-Jayne, "Mirror-Touch Synaesthesia," August 30, 2013. See http://syndiscovery.com/mirror-touch-synaesthesia/

Brindle, Kimberley, Richard Moulding, Kaitlyn Bakker, and Maja Nedeljkovic, "Is the Relationship between Sensory-Processing Sensitivity and Negative Affect Mediated by Emotional Regulation?" *Australian Journal of Psychology* (January 5, 2015). See http://onlinelibrary.wiley.com/doi/10.1111/ajpy.12084/abstract;jsessionid=E04B780D6D46141488C409109BC8FE54.f04t03?deniedAccessCustomisedMessage=&userIsAuthenticated=false

Davenport, Barrie, "5 Ways To Boost Emotional Intelligence In The Workplace." See http://liveboldandbloom.com/02/self-awareness-2/emotional-intelligence-workplace

Davenport, Barrie, "25 Action Steps for Transitioning to Your Life Passion," See http://liveboldandbloom.com/03/career/25-action-steps-for-transitioning-to-your-life-passion

Davenport, Barrie, "400 Value Words." See http://www.barriedavenport.com/list-of-400-values/

Davenport, Barrie, "Embrace Your Inner Adult." See http://liveboldandbloom.com/09/relationships/embrace-your-inner-adult

Davenport, Barrie, "The Path to Passion, Love What You Do." See http://pathtopassioncourse.com/

Davenport, Barrie, "How to Simplify Your Life: 50 Actions to Foster Peace and Contentment." See http://liveboldandbloom.com/

Davenport, Barrie, "Just a Bad Mood or Are You Coming Unglued?" See http://liveboldandbloom.com/10/health/just-a-bad-mood-or-are-you-coming-unglued

Davenport, Barrie, "Mindfulness Meditation: The Path to Inner Peace and Health." See http://liveboldandbloom.com/02/mindfulness/mindfulness-meditation

Davenport, Barrie, "Self-Awareness: 30 Essential Actions for Living Authentically." See http://liveboldandbloom.com/06/self-awareness-2/self-awareness

Davenport, Barrie, *The 52-Week Life Passion Project: Uncover Your Life Passion* and *Workbook* (Raleigh, North Carolina: Blue Elephant Press, 2012).

Face Research Lab, University of Glasgow, Scotland. See www.faceresearch.org

Gibran, Kahlil, *The Prophet* (New York: Alfred A. Knopf, 1973).

Holland, Julie, "Medicating Women's Feelings," *The New York Times* (February 29, 2015). See http://www.nytimes.com/2015/03/01/opinion/sunday/medicating-womens-feelings.html?_r=2

Iacoboni, Marco, *Mirroring People: The Science of Empathy and How We Connect with Others* (New York; Farrar, Straus, and Giroux, 2008), quote from 109, neuron reference from 4.

Jobin, Patrick, "The Definitive Guide to Choosing an Office Chair." See http://gearpatrol.com/2009/07/14/the-definitive-guide-to-choosing-an-office-chair/

Jung, Carl Gustav, *The Theory of Psychoanalysis* (New York: The Journal of Nervous and Mental Disease Publishing Company,1915), paragraphs 399, 398.

Kagan, Jerome. See http://en.wikipedia.org/wiki/Jerome_Kagan

Lebeau, Elise, "What Is an Empath?" See https://www.eliselebeau.com/

Messerschmidt, Peter, "HSP Topics: The Challenges of the Highly Sensitive Man" (June 11, 2015). See http://denmarkguy.hubpages.com/hub/HSP-Highly-Sensitive-Men

Oriah Mountain Dreamer, "The Invitation," *The Invitation* (New York: Harper Collins, 1999), 1–2.

Parramore, Lynn, "Are You a Highly Sensitive Person? Here's the Science behind this Personality Type" (December 23, 2014). See http://reset.me/story/highly-sensitive-person-need-know-science-personality-type/

Pincott, Jena, "Why Women Don't Want Macho Men," See http://www.wsj.com/articles/SB10001424052748704100604 4575145810050665030#MARK

Ramsey, Janine, "Highly Sensitive People in the Workplace—from Shame to Fame, January 2, 2014. See http://www.hrzone.com/perform/people/highly-sensitive-people-in-the-workplace-from-shame-to-fame

Scholten, Amy, "Dr. Elaine Aron on Highly Sensitive People in Relationships," CVS.com. See http://www.cvshealthresources.com/GetContent.aspx?token=f75979d3-9c7c-4b16-af56-3e122a3f19e3&chunkiid=14269

Sears, Williams Sears, "Twelve Features of a High Need Baby." See http://www.askdrsears.com/topics/health-concerns/fussy-baby/high-need-baby/high-needs-baby, and http://www.askdrsears.com/topics/health-concerns/fussy-baby/high-need-baby/12-features-high-need-baby

Seligman, Martin, and Steven F. Maier, "Failure to Escape Traumatic Shock," *Journal of Experimental Psychology,* 74 (May 1967).

Shrivastava, Bhavania, quoted in Janine Ramsey, "Highly Sensitive People in the Workplace—from Shame to Fame, January 2, 2014. See http://www.hrzone.com/perform/people/highly-sensitive-people-in-the-workplace-from-shame-to-fame

Zeff, Ted, "Healing the Highly Sensitive Male, August 2010. See http://www.hsperson.com/pages/2Aug10.htm

Zeff, Ted, The Highly Sensitive Person's Survival Guide: Essential Skills for Living Well in an Overstimulating World (Step-by-Step Guides) (Oakland, California: New Harbinger Publications, 2004).

Want to Learn More?

If you'd like to learn more about sensitivity, confidence and self-esteem, please visit my blog, Live Bold and Bloom.com, and check out my course, Simple Self-Confidence.com.

Did You Like *Finely Tuned*?

Thank you so much for purchasing *Finely Tuned*. I'm honored by the trust you've placed in me and my work by choosing this book to understand your sensitive traits. I truly hope you've enjoyed it and found it useful for your life.

I'd like to ask you for a small favor. Would you please take just a minute to leave a review for this book on Amazon? This feedback will help me continue to write the kind of books that will best serve you. If you really loved the book, please let me know!

Other Books You Might Enjoy from Barrie Davenport

Building Confidence: Get Motivated, Overcome Social Fear, Be Assertive, and Empower Your Life For Success

Peace of Mindfulness: Everyday Rituals to Conquer Anxiety and Claim Unlimited Inner Peace

Self-Discovery Questions: 155 Breakthrough Questions to Accelerate Massive Action

Confidence Hacks: 99 Small Actions to Massively Boost Your Confidence

10-Minute Declutter: The Stress-Free Habit for Simplifying Your Home

Sticky Habits: 6 Simple Steps To Create Good Habits That Stick

The 52-Week Life Passion Project: Uncover Your Life Passion

CPSIA information can be obtained at www.ICGtesting.com
Printed in the USA
LVOW10s1131060416

482416LV00001B/173/P

9 781515 023357